Collins

need to know?

Wine

Julie Arkell

Collins

First published in 2006 by Collins
an imprint of
HarperCollins Publishers
77–85 Fulham Palace Road
London W6 8JB

www.collins.co.uk

Collins is a registered trademark of
HarperCollins Publishers Limited.

10 09 08 07 06
6   5   4   3   2   1

A catalogue record for this book is available from
the British Library

Series design: Mark Thomson

Created by **Focus Publishing**, Sevenoaks, Kent
Project editor: Guy Croton
Designer: David Etherington
Front cover photograph: Getty Images/FoodPix/Bill Boch

ISBN-13 978 0 00 720468 7
ISBN-10 0 00 720468 X

Colour reproduction by Colourscan, Singapore
Printed and bound by Printing Express Ltd,
Hong Kong

Contents

Introduction

This book unashamedly flies in the face of tradition. Instead of classifying wines by country and region of origin, it turns everything upside down by looking at wines in terms of their styles and flavours and how best to appreciate them to the full.

A vineyard in New South Wales. Australian wines are hugely popular thanks to their up-front fruity flavours.

A matter of taste

To draw an analogy, think about how you would select an eating apple. Are you in the mood for something crunchy and tangy or do you crave a juicier, sweeter style? If you happened not to know the difference between the taste of, say, a Granny Smith and a Gala, how would you know which type of apple to buy? Furthermore, whilst you may prefer an English, New Zealand or South African apple, for example, chances are that you are not concerned about its precise origin as long as its flavour suits your taste.

It therefore makes sense to apply exactly the same logic when it comes to the challenging task of selecting a bottle of wine – and this is where this book comes into its own. Once you have decided on the style and flavour you want to drink, all you need to do is open these pages to discover a wealth of tasty recommendations.

How to use this book

Let us assume that you wish to buy a dry white wine. First of all, go to Chapter 3 and look at the general categories. Let us say that you fancy something with an aromatic personality – you now have to decide if you would prefer a delicate style or something with a more pungent or fruitier, floral character. Once you have narrowed down your choice, you will find a summary of the typical grapes from which these wines are crafted, where they are made and some specific names to look for. Finally, there is a handy section on what to eat with each style of wine.

At-a-glance guides
The main wine chapters contain a flavour trail and a country trail, which are useful if you are in a hurry. Respectively, these sum up at a glance where you can find your favourite style (by country and by region) and what each country and region does best.

Other useful information
Apart from providing you with all the information you need to help you choose wine with a new-found confidence, this book also features plenty of practical advice, from how to start a wine cellar to how to throw a good wine party. Additionally, if you are keen to learn more about the nuts and bolts of viticulture (what goes on in the vineyard) and/or vinification (the winemaking process), all the basic information can be found in these pages.

A winery worker takes a break during the busy harvesting and winemaking season.

Wine country and region maps
You will find a number of maps distributed throughout the book, which also provide a brief summary of the country or countries they portray and highlight their principal wine regions. As far as possible, these maps have been placed alongside the type and colour of wine with which they are most closely associated.

1 From grape to glass

If you think about it, it seems somewhat amazing that grapes – a tiny fruit – are responsible for creating such a profusion and variety of wine styles. Yet these humble berries first and foremost determine the smell and taste of any wine. Where and how they are grown, and the way in which they are manipulated, have a profound effect on quality and flavour. Even a rudimentary grasp of these principles will help you choose wine with extra confidence.

Grape expectations

Nature provides the key ingredient of flavour in the form of the grape and one of the fastest ways of learning more about wine is to become familiar with the styles that each variety creates.

The versatile Semillon grape makes both sweet and dry white wines.

Top 15 grape varieties

► **Cabernet Sauvignon**

Creates mainly: fruity reds. Typical aromas/flavours: blackcurrants; cherry; blackberry; chocolate; black pepper; green olives; mint; eucalyptus; cedar, pencil shavings; cigar box.

► **Chardonnay**

Creates mainly: neutral whites; richer, bolder whites; sparkling wines. Typical aromas/flavours: lemon; melon; nuts (unoaked); butterscotch; tropical fruit; spice; cream (oaked).

► **Chenin Blanc**

Creates mainly: neutral whites; richer, bolder whites; tangy whites; sweet whites. Typical aromas/flavours: apples; hay; beeswax; almonds; wet wool; guava; melon; pear; fig.

► **Gamay**

Creates mainly: easy-drinking reds. Typical aromas/flavours: red cherries; bananas; raspberries; strawberries; plums; bubble gum.

► **Grenache/Garnacha**

Creates mainly: fruity reds; rosés. Typical aromas/flavours: black and red fruits; smoke; nuts; white pepper; toffee; chocolate; leather; mud; coffee.

► **Merlot**

Creates mainly: fruity reds. Typical aromas/flavours: brambles; damsons; blackcurrants; chocolate; black cherries; pepper; cigar box; mint; coffee beans.

▶ **Muscat**
Creates mainly: aromatic whites; sweet whites; sparkling wines. Typical aromas/flavours: crunchy green grapes (dry; sweet sparkling); marmalade (sweet; fortified).

▶ **Pinot Noir**
Creates mainly: mellow reds; sparkling whites. Typical aromas/flavours: strawberry; raspberry; plum; cherry; truffles; game.

▶ **Riesling**
Creates mainly: tangy whites; sweet whites. Typical aromas/flavours: floral; peach; apple; lime; honey; kerosene.

▶ **Sangiovese**
Creates mainly: powerful reds. Typical aromas/flavours: violets; plums; earth; tobacco, leather; herbs; tea leaves.

▶ **Sauvignon Blanc**
Creates mainly: tangy whites; richer, bolder whites. Typical aromas/flavours: gooseberries; nettles; elderflower; tomato leaf; asparagus; freshly sliced green capsicum; grapefruit.

▶ **Sémillon/Semillon**
Creates mainly: richer, bolder whites; sweet whites. Typical aromas/flavours: grassy; citrus fruit; lime cordial; fig; pear; greengages; melon (young); honey; custardy; nuts (mature).

▶ **Syrah/Shiraz**
Creates mainly: powerful reds. Typical aromas/flavours: violets; leather; wild berries; ripe plums; liquorice; black pepper; chocolate.

▶ **Tempranillo**
Creates mainly: fruity reds. Typical aromas/flavours: black fruits; strawberries; brown sugar; cocoa; vanilla; spice; pipe tobacco; herbs.

▶ **Zinfandel/Primitivo**
Creates mainly: powerful reds; rosés. Typical aromas/flavours: blackberries; raspberries; red cherry; dried fruit; mixed spice; dates; mint; black pepper.

Tempranillo grapes growing on the vine in northern Spain.

In the vineyard

Wine producers around the world have recognized that top quality wine cannot be made without top quality grapes. To this end, new heights of viticultural technology have been pioneered, from the moment the vine is propagated in the nursery to the manner in which the grapes are delivered to the winery.

The basic requirements

For centuries, soil, climate, altitude, topography, aspect and availability of water have all been taken into consideration when choosing a vineyard site – and nothing has changed today. Careful attention is also paid to selecting suitable varieties, and the density of planting of the vines, the method of pruning and training, and when the grapes are picked are equally critical. All of the above combine to shape the character of the grapes

Whatever the equipment used to harvest them, there is no substitute for fine grapes grown on good soil.

produced and, in turn, the kind of wine to which they give birth. But let us examine a few of these factors in more detail.

Soil
Each grape variety has its own demands as far as soil is concerned – Chardonnay, say, grows best in limestone, while Syrah prefers granite and Riesling adores slate. In general, though, top grapes come from vines planted in infertile, free-draining soils where they are forced to plunge their roots deep into the ground in search of life-giving water and nutrients.

Climate
This also dictates what grapes are cultivated where. Some varieties need plenty of hot sunshine to ripen and are therefore unsuitable for cool climates, whereas others relish the struggle that marginal conditions confer. A model wine climate calls for a frost- and hail-free spring, a warm, dry summer, a long, slow ripening season, a rain-free harvest and a chilly winter.

Altitude, topography and aspect
Elevated slopes attract more hours of sunshine than flat land, particularly if they are facing the Equator. Furthermore, in hot countries, the best vineyards are found high up on valley slopes where the weather is beneficially cooler. Proximity to a large mass of water is important in marginal climates as it helps to modify cold temperatures, especially by providing protection against damaging spring frosts.

Irrigation
Vast stretches of vineyards (particularly in the New World) rely heavily on irrigation during the growing season – indeed, the vines could not be cultivated without it. However, the amount of water supplied to the vines must be handled with care. The quality of the crop – and hence the quality of the wine it makes – suffers when the vineyards are over-irrigated.

Pruning and training

Most vines are trained along a wire trellis. The idea behind this practice is to expose the leaves to plenty of sunshine so that enough energy is generated to grow the grapes and ripen them. In cool climates, however, grapes will not ripen if they are over-shaded by the foliage, whereas in hot climates, they may be scorched if the canopy is not dense enough. The density and spacing of the vines themselves is also important in controlling yields.

Reaping the rewards

The timing of the harvest is also crucial. Most producers desire fully ripened grapes packed full of sugar for rich, flavoursome wines. Some styles, however, require grapes with low sugar levels.

Very cold weather actually assists vines by killing bugs and allowing them to rest.

The vineyard cycle

Winter – Key events: pruning. Ideal conditions: cold weather to force the vines to rest and to kill off bugs.
Spring – Key events: bud burst; leaf growth; weed control; training new shoots to the trellising wires. Ideal conditions: no frost or hail which can destroy vulnerable young buds.
Summer – Key events: flowering; fruit set into clusters that become grapes; leaf-plucking to expose the grapes to more sunlight; véraison (the fruit changes colour); green harvesting to remove excess fruit. Ideal conditions: warm, dry and sunny, with a long, slow ripening season.
Autumn – Key events: harvest (usually September/October in the northern hemisphere and February/March in the southern hemisphere). Ideal conditions: no rain to dilute the grapes before they are picked.

In the winery

Modern winemaking is all about squeezing top quality wines from top quality grapes. We have seen that flavour comes from the latter, though as we will soon appreciate, actions in the winery also have a massive role to play in bringing out – and protecting – this precious commodity.

Winemaking in six easy steps

1. The stems are removed and the grapes are crushed to break their skins and release the juice.

2. The grape juice is pumped into stainless steel, concrete or fibreglass tanks, though oak barrels or casks are the vessel of choice for premium wines. Yeasts (either wild yeasts present on the grape skins and in the atmosphere, or more predictable, laboratory-cultured strains inoculated into the juice) convert the grape sugars into alcohol and carbon dioxide – this is alcoholic fermentation. It comes to a grinding halt when the yeasts die because they have gobbled up all of the sugars, delivering wine that is dry in taste.

The modern winery is a high-tech environment featuring a wide range of specialist equipment.

3. Malolactic fermentation is a secondary, bacterial fermentation that turns harsh malic acid (from *malum*, the Latin for apple) to the softer lactic acid (from *lactis*, the Latin for milk) and carbon dioxide. This can occur spontaneously, or may be induced via an injection of lactic bacteria. If the 'malo' is not wanted, the new wine is immediately filtered off its lees (sediment formed by dead yeast cells and other by-products of alcoholic fermentation) and is protected against any further bacterial invasion.

must know

Chaptalization
Cane or beet sugar,
or concentrated
grape juice, is
sometimes added
before or during
fermentation to
raise the alcohol
level in the
finished wine. This
practice is
common in cool
climate countries
where grapes
cannot always
ripen fully.

4. Premium wines are usually aged in 225-litre/50-gallon oak barriques (the posh name for barrels). White wines spend an average of six to eight months in barrel, compared with an average of nine to eighteen months for reds.

5. Wines made from various grape varieties, or from different batches of the same crop that have been vinified separately, may be blended together. Contrary to popular belief, blended wines are not inferior to varietal wines (those made from a single grape variety). Indeed, many of the world's famous wine names are blends.

6. The wine is filtered to take it off its lees and is then fined to chemically remove unwanted solids (proteins, yeasts and other organic particles) held in suspension. This stabilizes it and improve clarity. The wine is now bottled.

Taking the temperature

Temperature control is the single most important factor in winemaking, particularly in countries where the grapes ripen and the wines are made under a red hot sun. In these circumstances, the management of temperature commences from the moment the grapes are picked and the fruit is rushed to the winery as quickly as possible, often in refrigerated trucks. Indeed, harvesting is often carried out at night when everything, including the grapes, is much cooler. But this safeguard is pointless if the temperature generated during fermentation is allowed to run wild – low temperatures are central to preserving aroma, freshness and fruit flavours in white wines in particular.

In cool climate countries, low ambient temperatures in autumn keep fermentation temperatures in check quite naturally. In places where the weather is still sizzling at time of harvest, temperatures must be moderated artificially. If the wine is to be made in barrels, they need to be stored in an air-conditioned environment. Other fermentation vessels, especially stainless steel tanks, are specially designed to cool

A bottling line in a
contemporary
winery.

the wine inside them by dribbling cold water down their
sides within an additional internal skin. It works!

A breath of fresh air

When fresh, clean, everyday wines are wanted, it is vital that
air is excluded from every part of the winemaking operation
because air contains oxygen, and oxygen is the arch enemy
of wine. Protective, 'reductive' measures begin the instant
the grapes are picked by blanketing them in inert gas. For
premium styles, however, the winemaker may choose to
expose the juice to a small amount of air prior to
fermentation. The wine develops beneficial nuances of
flavour as a result of this 'oxidative' exercise.

**Enormous stainless
steel barrels are a
feature of just about
any winery these
days, although oak
barrels are still the
vessel of choice
for premium
winemaking.**

Ageing well

Simple, easy-drinking wines for immediate drinking are bottled
as soon as they are made. Many wines, however, benefit from a

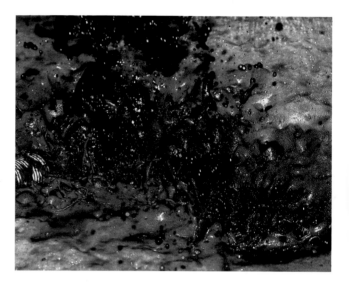

Wine goes through many different stages before it becomes the refined liquid you pour at your table.

period of ageing. This is required to soften tannins and acids – substances used in the manufacturing process to make the wine more mellow. The storage medium in which this takes place – and the length of time the wine spends in it – has an enormous impact on flavour.

There are two sorts of ageing: in wood and in bottle. Some wines are kept in wood for a while and are then ready to drink – Rioja, tawny port and sherry, for instance, fit this bill. Others need a combination of time in wood followed by time in bottle before they can be drunk – vintage port and top wines from Bordeaux and Burgundy are examples that fall into this category.

Needless to say, bottles are made from glass, a neutral material that does not add or take away anything in terms of flavour, although wine continues to evolve in it nevertheless. Wood is very different from glass: it interacts with the wine and the timber chosen, the size of the cask and the way it has been treated all affect flavour. You can discover more on the next page.

Understanding oak

It is an extraordinary fact that oak is just about the only type of wood that is exploited in quality winemaking. No other genus has demonstrated such a natural affinity with wine.

Why oak?

Oak is strong, supple and watertight and is used to assemble the barrels in which premium wines are fermented and/or matured. The wine saps tannin, flavour and colour from the oak, and because the wood is porous, it allows the wine to breathe, causing further complex changes to its chemical make-up.

The attributes of oaked wine are influenced by the age of the wood and the size of the barrel and the longer the time the wine spends in it, the greater the power the oak will have.

The most-prized oak comes from the French forests of Alliers, Limousin, Nevers, Tronçais and Vosges. American oak, which gives a much sweeter and stronger vanilla taste, is also popular, especially in Australia, Rioja and the Americas. Where and how the staves of wood are seasoned is also pivotal, as is the degree of charring the inside of the barrel receives when it is being constructed.

Despite centuries of experimentation with other woods – from acacia to walnut – oak is the only genus that lends itself to successful winemaking.

Wine around the world

Looking at the shelves, it would be natural to assume that wine is made everywhere. In reality, though, most vines cannot tolerate extremes of heat or cold and are therefore cultivated only between the latitudes of 30° and 50°N, and 30° and 40°S.

Major wine-producing countries					
Country	Best known for	Key grapes	Key sources	Quality	World ranking
Argentina	Reds and whites	Bonarda; Cabernet Sauvignon; Chardonnay; Chenin Blanc; Malbec; Merlot; Sauvignon Blanc; Syrah; Torrontés	La Rioja; Mendoza; Río Negro; Salta; San Juan	Very good	5
Australia	Reds and whites	Cabernet Sauvignon; Chardonnay; Grenache; Pinot Noir; Riesling; Sauvignon Blanc; Shiraz; Viognier	New South Wales; South Australia; Tasmania; Victoria; Western Australia	Excellent	6
Chile	Reds and whites	Cabernet Sauvignon; Carmenère; Chardonnay; Merlot; Pinot Noir; Sauvignon Blanc; Syrah	Aconcagua; Bío-Bío; Cachapoal; Casablanca; Colchagua; Curicó; Maipo; Maule; San Antonio Valley	Excellent	10
France	All styles	Cabernet Franc; Cabernet Sauvignon; Chardonnay; Chenin Blanc; Cinsault;	Alsace; Bordeaux; Burgundy; Champagne;	Excellent	1

Major wine-producing countries

Country	Best known for	Key grapes	Key sources	Quality	World ranking
		Gamay; Grenache; Malbec; Merlot; Mourvèdre; Muscat; Pinot Noir; Sauvignon Blanc; Sémillon; Syrah; Viognier	Loire; Rhône; south; southwest		
Germany	Whites and sweeties	Gewürztraminer; Grauburgunder; Riesling; Scheurebe; Silvaner	Baden; Mosel-Saar-Ruwer; Nahe; Pfalz; Rheingau; Rheinhessen	Excellent	7
Italy	Reds, whites and sparkling	Aglianico; Barbera; Cabernet Sauvignon; Chardonnay; Corvina; Dolcetto; Lagrein; Malvasia; Merlot; Montepulciano; Muscat; Nebbiolo; Negroamaro; Nero d'Avola; Pinot Grigio; Primitivo; Sangiovese; Trebbiano; Verdicchio	Friuli-Venezia Giulia; Lombardia; Marche; Piemonte; Puglia; Trentino-Alto Adige; Tuscany; Sicily; Veneto	Excellent	2
New Zealand	Reds, whites and sparkling	Cabernet Sauvignon; Chardonnay; Merlot; Pinot Noir; Sauvignon Blanc	Auckland; Canterbury; Central Otago; Gisborne; Hawkes Bay; Marlborough; Martinborough; Nelson; Northland; Wellington	Excellent	33

1 From grape to glass

Major wine-producing countries					
Country	Best known for	Key grapes	Key sources	Quality	World ranking
Portugal	All styles except sparkling	Baga; Fernão Pires; Periquita; Touriga Francesca; Touriga Nacional; Trincadeira	Alentejo; Bairrada; Dão; Douro; Estremadura; Ribatejo; Terras do Sado; Vinho Verde	Excellent	8
South Africa	Reds and whites	Cabernet Sauvignon; Chardonnay; Chenin Blanc; Colombard; Merlot; Pinotage; Sauvignon Blanc; Shiraz	Constantia; Franschhoek; Little Karoo; Malmesbury; Olifants River; Orange River; Paarl; Robertson; Stellenbosch; Walker Bay; Worcester	Excellent	9
Spain	All styles	Airén; Albariño; Bobal; Garnacha; Monastrell; Tempranillo	Costers del Segre; La Mancha; Navarra; Penedès; Rías Baixas; Ribera del Duero; Rioja; Rueda; Somontano	Excellent	3
USA	Reds and whites	Cabernet Sauvignon; Chardonnay; Merlot; Pinot Noir; Riesling; Sauvignon Blanc; Syrah; Zinfandel	California; New York State; Oregon and Washington State	Excellent	4

Other wine-producing countries

There are very few countries in the world that do not make wine of some kind. Outside the main wine-producing countries featured in the table on the preceding pages, good wine is also made in Austria, Canada, the Czech Republic, England and Wales, Greece, Hungary, Lebanon, Mexico, Switzerland and Uruguay. However, be careful of Bulgarian, Moroccan, Romanian and Slovakian wines which are not renowned for their quality.

Also-rans

Whilst wine (some of it drinkable!) is also produced in the following countries, very little, if any, is exported: Algeria; Armenia; Azerbaijan; Bohemia; Bosnia-Herzegovina; Brazil; China; Croatia; Cyprus; Georgia; India; Israel; Japan; Kazakhstan; Luxembourg; Macedonia; Moldova; Montenegro; Peru; Russia; Serbia; Slovenia; Tunisia; Turkey; Ukraine.

In some parts of the world, traditional methods of crushing grapes are still deployed.

Eco-friendly wines

An increasing awareness of the environment around us has prompted many consumers to demand wines that are made to more exacting standards with regard to land management.

Modern winemaking involves the use of machinery, yet organic and biodynamic principles are sometimes applied to the process.

Organic wines

These are produced from grapes grown without the use of chemical fertilizers, pesticides, fungicides and herbicides. Instead, soil is nourished by compost, animal manure and discarded vine prunings, grape skins and pips, and nitrogen is provided by cover crops such as clover and mustard.

Biodynamic viticulture

Based on theories promulgated by Rudolf Steiner, this innovation takes organic viticulture one step further. The rules of biodynamic viticulture are far stricter, particularly regarding what is added to the soil (which is viewed as an organism in its own right) and when it is applied. Indeed, the timing of all vineyard activity is governed by the phases of the moon, the movement of the stars and planets and other cosmic rhythms. This may sound strange, but it does work!

Sustainable viticulture/integrated management

Completely dismissing chemical treatments can often prove an economic risk in cold, damp regions where fungal diseases such as mildew and grey rot (that can easily wipe out a year's crop) are prevalent. Many growers therefore compromise by reducing their use to the bare minimum and only when absolutely necessary.

Vegetarian wines

It is natural to assume that vegetarians and vegans can drink any wine: after all, how can wine have any connection with animals (apart from those that love eating the grapes in the vineyard...)?

The truth of the matter

The plain fact is that animal or fish products have been exploited in winemaking for centuries, most specifically in the fining process, which helps clear the wine of unwanted solids held in suspension. The fining agents used can be isinglass (derived from the swim bladders of certain fish, most notably sturgeon), gelatin (the result of cooking bones, tendons, skins and connective tissue, rather like making stock from a chicken carcass), modified casein (which comes from milk), chitin (obtained from shellfish and crustaceans), egg whites, or (in the past, admittedly) ox blood. Absolutely nothing of the fining agent remains in the wine after it has been filtered, but this is not the point!

Animal-friendly alternatives

Fortunately, many producers use non-animal substances to fine their wines, such as bentonite and kieselguhr (both types of diatomaceous earth), so these can be drunk with a clear conscience. Unfortunately, the only way of knowing if the wine is suitable is by scrutinizing the back label for this kind of information and even then it might only say 'suitable for vegetarians', which is of no use whatsoever to vegans if, say, egg white or casein has been used in the manufacturing process.

want to know more?

Take it to the next level...

- ▶ **Understanding the label** 28
- ▶ **How white wines are made** 44
- ▶ **How red wines are made** 80
- ▶ **How rosé wines are made** 122

Other sources

- ▶ Invest in a book that specializes in grape varieties, such as *Grapes & Wines* by Oz Clarke and Margaret Rand (Websters/Little, Brown & Company, 2001).
- ▶ Compare unoaked and oaked versions of the same wine, from the same producer and from the same vintage (Australian Chardonnay, for example).
- ▶ For more information on where wine is made, buy *The World Atlas of Wine* (Mitchell Beazley, 2001) by Hugh Johnson and Jancis Robinson.

Weblinks

- ▶ For more information on winemaking, visit: www.decanter.com www.wine-regions-of-the-world.com www.centurywine.8m.com

2 Appreciating the flavours

Is it possible to know what a wine is going to taste like short of pulling the cork out of the bottle and actually drinking it? Happily, the answer is yes. This chapter demonstrates how you can interpret the many clues to flavour provided on the label and also examines the ways by which you can maximize every wine-drinking experience. Last but not least, there is a host of tips on venturing further into a whole new world of exciting and rewarding flavours.

Understanding the label

As you learn how to decipher the information on wine bottle labels, you will quickly realize that they can be an invaluable tool when it comes to the business of selecting wine.

The grape variety
Search for the name of the grape(s) from which the wine has been made. Each grape has its own signature, so it is clear that when you arm yourself with the knowledge of their individual characteristics, you are better equipped to predict the style of wine in the bottle. There is one big snag, however. The name of the grape(s) often does not appear on the labels of traditional Old World wines!

The country and region of origin
Progress in vineyard husbandry and state-of-the-art winemaking techniques mean that modern wines are usually well-made wherever they come from. But one factor that even top producers cannot control is climate, which has a huge impact on the overall style of any wine. For example, a white wine made from Chardonnay in a cool region has a restrained, lemony, mineral style, while Chardonnays from hot vineyards are fat and creamy, oozing lush, sunshine-ripe, tropical fruit flavours. It takes time – and a lot of comparative tasting! – to get to grips with the variations between the wines of each country and each region, but as a rule, expect Old World wines to be more austere compared with those from the New World. This is to say that they are generally more restrained in style.

The vintage
A label showing a vintage means that the wine has been made from grapes harvested in that year. Vintages are of concern only

in regions with marginal climates where the crop is truly at the mercy of nature. If the grapes do not ripen properly, the wine they make tastes unpleasantly green and harsh.

Oak

Does the label state that the wine been fermented and/or aged in oak? The significance of oak has been discussed in the previous chapter, but it is worth repeating that oak makes vast changes to the taste of the finished wine. You can be assured that it is going to be more serious (and more expensive!), with deeper, richer and weightier flavours. Key words to look for on the label are oaked, oak aged, *fûts de chêne*, barrel fermented, barrel aged, *riserva*, *reserva* and *crianza*.

Some grape varieties need a hot climate, while others relish the struggle of marginal conditions.

must know

Beware of misleading terms
Words such as 'superior', 'premium', 'special', 'classic' and 'limited release' may promise a lot, but they can be meaningless. Indeed, be aware that absolutely nothing that is written on the label guarantees the quality of the liquid in the bottle.

Alcoholic strength

This is expressed as a percentage of total volume in the bottle and generally reflects the ripeness of the grapes at the time of picking – the riper they are, the more sugar there is available for conversion into alcohol during fermentation. Alcohol gives a mouth-warming feeling, a slightly sweet and oily taste and, of course, the potential hangover!

Back labels and taste indicators

Many consumer-friendly producers also paste a back label onto the bottle. Not unexpectedly, these regularly feature glowing praise for the wine inside, but if you can cut through the marketing hype, you may uncover some genuinely worthwhile information. In particular, check to see if there is a symbol that offers a guide to the sweetness of white wine (measured on a scale of one to nine, with one being bone dry) and for reds, how light- or full-bodied it is (on a scale of A to E, A is the lightest-bodied style).

Back labels sometimes also provide recommendations for suitable food matches and for how long the wine should be kept, though it is a good idea to be suspicious of the latter. Always ensure that you buy your wine from an outlet which has a healthy turnover of stock.

Brands

A lot of snobbishness surrounds brands; for example, Jacob's Creek is a popular yet perfectly good wine which attracts some derision. Some of them are over-priced, admittedly, but most are tasty and, moreover, are reliable. If you are faced with a sea of unknown wines, a brand may prove to be the most prudent buy.

Specialist wine terminology

Unfortunately, wine is not exempt from specialist jargon. Although much 'wine speak' refers to viticulture (growing the grapes) and vinification (making the wine), some of the language relates to taste and you will find it helpful to become acquainted with these terms as you learn more about wine.

Some commonly used words

Balance: a well-balanced wine is one in which sweetness, acidity, fruit, tannin and alcohol are all in perfect harmony.

Body: the weight and texture of the wine in the mouth. A 'heavy' wine is termed full-bodied whereas a light-bodied wine is, well, lighter! To draw a useful comparison, think of the difference between a vodka and tonic and a creamy liqueur.

Finish: also called length, describes the taste that lingers in your mouth after you have swallowed. Wines with a 'long' or 'good' finish are those where the after-taste persists for some time (a positive effect). If the flavour disappears quickly, it has a 'short' finish.

Nose: another name for the smell of wine.

Palate: the technical term for taste.

Describing wine

It makes absolute sense to compare the aroma and taste of wine with the flavours of anything found in the fruit bowl ... on a plate ... in the kitchen ... in the garden ... during a country walk ... and then to use these associations to describe it. Apart from anything else, your tasting notes will mean something to you when you look back on them.

You don't need to know jargon in order to enjoy wine, but a few key terms will enhance the experience.

Label lessons

The information supplied on the label of a bottle of wine is very often specific to a particular country or even region. Here is a brief guide to the main terms to be found on the world's wines.

Côtes de Beaune-Villages, Appellation Contrôlée (AC or AOC) Appellation (d'Origine) Contrôlée (AC or AOC) is the official quality designation that guarantees origin and minimum standards of production. It can cover anything from a whole region to an individual vineyard.

Tells us that the company was founded in 1859.

French wine labels

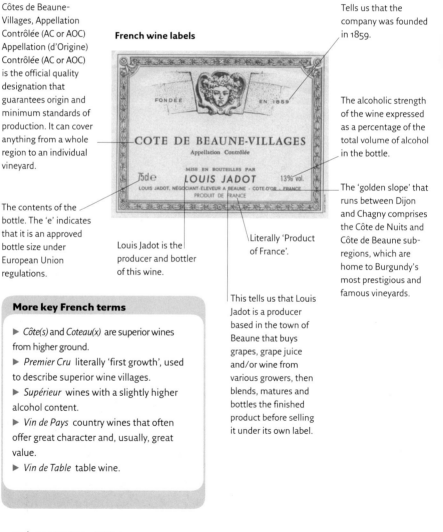

The alcoholic strength of the wine expressed as a percentage of the total volume of alcohol in the bottle.

The 'golden slope' that runs between Dijon and Chagny comprises the Côte de Nuits and Côte de Beaune sub-regions, which are home to Burgundy's most prestigious and famous vineyards.

The contents of the bottle. The 'e' indicates that it is an approved bottle size under European Union regulations.

Louis Jadot is the producer and bottler of this wine.

Literally 'Product of France'.

This tells us that Louis Jadot is a producer based in the town of Beaune that buys grapes, grape juice and/or wine from various growers, then blends, matures and bottles the finished product before selling it under its own label.

More key French terms

▶ *Côte(s)* and *Coteau(x)* are superior wines from higher ground.
▶ *Premier Cru* literally 'first growth', used to describe superior wine villages.
▶ *Supérieur* wines with a slightly higher alcohol content.
▶ *Vin de Pays* country wines that often offer great character and, usually, great value.
▶ *Vin de Table* table wine.

Herrenberg is the name of an individual vineyard located in the village of Oppenheim. Riesling is the name of the grape. Auslese means that the wine has been made from selected bunches of very ripe grapes.

This means that the wine has been bottled at the Louis Guntrum estate, based in the town of Nierstein.

Literally a top quality wine 'with distinction', progressively classified by natural grape ripeness as Kabinett, Spätlese, Auslese, Beerenauslese, Eiswein and Trockenbeerenauslese.

The name of the producer.

Tells us that the company was founded in 1648.

The vintage, i.e. the year in which the grapes were harvested.

The alcoholic strength of the wine expressed as a percentage of the total volume of alcohol in the bottle.

The contents of the bottle.

The region of production.

The Amtliche Prüfungsnummer (A. P. Number) is a government testing number found on all quality (QbA and QmP) labels that shows that they have passed rigorous laboratory and tasting checks.

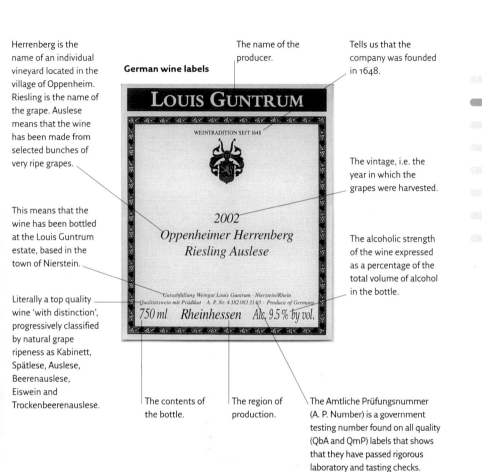

German wine labels

LOUIS GUNTRUM

WEINTRADITION SEIT 1648

2002
Oppenheimer Herrenberg
Riesling Auslese

Gutsabfüllung Weingut Louis Guntrum · Nierstein/Rhein
Qualitätswein mit Prädikat - A. P. Nr. 4 382 083 31 03 · Produce of Germany

750 ml   Rheinhessen   Alc. 9.5 % by vol.

More key German terms

▶ *Classic* everyday dry white made from a single grape variety and with regional typicity.
▶ *Deutscher Landwein* country wine that must be *trocken* or *halbtrocken*.
▶ *Deutscher Tafelwein* table wine.
▶ *Qualitätswein bestimmter Anbaugebiete* (QbA) official German quality designation that guarantees origin and minimum standards of production.

More key Italian terms

▶ *Classico* wines that hail from the historical heartland of a wine region. Wines described as 'X Classico' are generally considered better than just 'X'.

▶ *Denominazione di Origine Controllata* (DOC) official Italian quality designation that guarantees origin and minimum standards of production.

▶ *Denominazione di Origine Controllata e Garantita* (DOCG) the designation reserved for the very best Italian wines.

▶ *Superiore* wines with a slightly higher alcohol content than is normal for any given appellation. Beware! It does not mean that they are superior in taste!

▶ *Vino da Tavola* table wine. The most humble of Italian wine appellations, but nevertheless very often an indicator of a perfectly pleasant and drinkable wine.

Italian wine labels

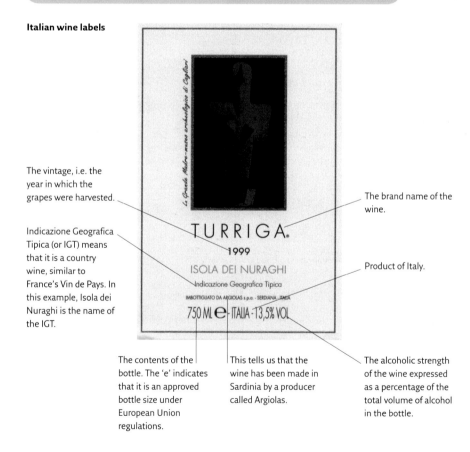

The vintage, i.e. the year in which the grapes were harvested.

The brand name of the wine.

Indicazione Geografica Tipica (or IGT) means that it is a country wine, similar to France's Vin de Pays. In this example, Isola dei Nuraghi is the name of the IGT.

Product of Italy.

The contents of the bottle. The 'e' indicates that it is an approved bottle size under European Union regulations.

This tells us that the wine has been made in Sardinia by a producer called Argiolas.

The alcoholic strength of the wine expressed as a percentage of the total volume of alcohol in the bottle.

Spanish wine labels

The name of the wine.

Tells us that the company was founded in 1879.

This means that the wine has been aged for a minimum period in oak and in bottle.

The name of the producer.

The alcoholic strength of the wine expressed as a percentage of the total volume of alcohol in the bottle.

13% Vol.
75 cl. e
R.E.N° 44.VI

embotellado por

Compañia Vinicola del Norte de España, s.a.

HARO-ESPAÑA
Embotellado en Laguardia

RIOJA
Denominación de origen calificada

PRODUCIDO EN ESPAÑA

This tells us that the wine was bottled in the town of Laguardia.

Product of Spain.

The contents of the bottle. The 'e' indicates that it is an approved bottle size under European Union regulations.

COSECHA 1999

Cosecha means vintage, so this means that all the grapes for this wine were harvested in 1999.

This quality designation is reserved for the very best Spanish wines.

The region of production.

More key Spanish terms

▶ *Crianza* wine aged for a minimum of two years, including at least six months in oak.
▶ *Denominacíon de Origen* (DOC) official quality designation that guarantees origin and minimum standards of production.
▶ *Gran Reserva* wine aged for a minimum of five years, including at least two in oak.
▶ *Joven* young wine with little or no ageing in oak.
▶ *Vino Comarcal* (VC) regional wine.
▶ *Vino de la Mesa* table wine.
▶ *Vino de la Tierra* country wine.

Taking the temperature

Take a few seconds to imagine the contrast in flavour between hot, juicy, roasted chicken fresh from the oven and cold, dry, next-day leftovers which have been sitting in the fridge. You will therefore not be surprised to read that the taste and character of wine also depends on the temperature at which it is served.

Chill white, rosé and sparkling wines

These styles are lifeless and unrefreshing if they are served too warm. The textbook temperature is around 7°C/45°F – but not everyone owns a wine thermometer. To be more practical, this equates to an hour or two in the door of the fridge. Once you have opened the wine, keep it chilled in a vacuum bottle cooler.

How to chill wine quickly

▶ Place the bottle in the freezer for ten minutes or so. This is very effective and does not harm the wine at all (though be

An ice bucket is the traditional device for keeping champagne and other wines chilled.

warned that sparkling wines have a tendency to explode if you forget about them!).

▶ Immerse the bottle in an ice bucket, washing-up bowl or sink, filled with ice, water and a handful of salt and leave it there for around 15 minutes. If you are throwing a party and have lots of wine to chill, you could even use the bath!

▶ Place the wine outdoors in cold weather.

▶ Invest in a reusable, gel-based, flexible sleeve that you keep in the freezer at all times. Slip it over the bottle and the wine will become cool within five minutes.

must know

A beach party tip
Keep wine cool by exercising the laws of physics and evaporation. Dunk towels in the sea, wrap them around the bottles and then leave them to dry in the sun.

Serve reds at room temperature

Now here is a conundrum: exactly what does 'room temperature' mean? Red wines do not favour the hothouse conditions of a centrally-heated home located in a cold climate region. Then again, the icy blasts of air conditioning required for comfort in hotter areas is not perfect, either! As a rule of thumb, red wines should be served at a temperature of around 15 °C/59 °F, but once more, you do not have to measure the temperature precisely! All you really need to remember is that cold reds have a hard, tannic bite, whilst over-warmed reds taste stewed.

How to warm wine quickly

▶ Pour the wine into a glass and then cradle it between your hands.

▶ Put the bottle into a container filled with lukewarm water and leave it for ten minutes.

▶ If you own a microwave with a digital timer, decant the wine into a jug, choose a low power setting and then heat the wine, almost second by second, erring on the side of caution and testing the temperature at the end of each cycle. You need strong nerves for this tricky task, but it can work well!

You can now buy wine coolers and heaters which will ensure that you serve your wine at precisely the right temperature.

Wine-tasting skills

If you acquire the habit of analyzing what you are drinking, you will soon discover that you are perceiving a wider range of aromas and flavours and that your ability to evaluate wine quality has become greatly enhanced.

Take a close look at the wine in the glass before you put it to your lips. There are plenty of visual clues.

Observe and inspect

Have a good look at the wine. Apart from checking that it does not show any obvious visible faults (cloudy wine, for example, is probably not fit to drink), much can be learned from a quick study of its colour and opacity. Young/bone-dry/simple white wines are usually pale and watery-looking, which suggests they are light-bodied in style. Older/sweeter/more complex whites are more golden in hue and appear more viscous, indicating that they are richer to taste. Red wines are vividly purple when they are newly-made, turning from ruby to garnet to tawny as they age. You can judge the weight of reds by looking into the wine – if you can see the bottom of the glass, the wine is light-bodied; if you cannot, it is full-bodied. It really is as simple as that.

Have a sniff

It is time to put your olfactory nerves to work. Make sure there is enough room in the glass for you to be able to stick your nose in for a jolly good sniff without getting it wet. Now vigorously swirl the wine around the glass. All this churning and eddying breaks up the molecules and releases aroma – relishing the smell of wine is part of the joy of drinking it. Of what does it remind you? It could be elderflower, mint, raspberries or coal tar. As we saw in Chapter 1, you are smelling the primary character of the grape variety, though as your knowledge grows, you will begin to pick up other scents that may provide evidence about how the wine has been made.

Testing those taste buds

Take a sip of the wine. But instead of swallowing it (which is your natural instinct), hold it in your mouth and let the liquid roll over, around and under your tongue. Now 'chew' the wine so that it coats your gums and hits all the parts of the mouth responsible for sending taste sensation messages to the brain – it allows you to appreciate its full flavour. If you can, simultaneously suck in a little air to aerate the wine, which brings out its taste even further.

What to think about

How dry or sweet is it? Is this the result of residual sugar or grape ripeness? Does it make your mouth water? If so, the wine is packed with natural acidity. Does a red wine make your mouth pucker? This is the effect of tannin. How much body and alcohol does it have? Has the wine been in contact with oak? The age of the wine also affects flavour. Young wines flaunt fruitiness; older wines are more mellow. Assess balance, finish and whether or not the flavour matched up to the promise of aroma. And, of course, ask yourself if you like it! Finally, always jot down a few tasting notes – our memory for taste is incredibly fickle.

An appreciation of the scent of wine – its 'bouquet' – is central to all wine tasting.

Recognizing faulty wine

Your nose is your best weapon of defence here. If a wine does not smell wholesome and appetizing when you first open the bottle, then neither is it likely to taste wholesome and appetizing!

An accumulation of tartrate crystals in a wine bottle is nothing to worry about.

Corked wine

Thanks to the cork-contaminating compound 2, 4, 6-Trichloroanisole, it is estimated that as many as one in 15 bottles of wine sealed with a natural cork may be ruined by a truly offensive, musty odour reminiscent of dirty bird cages, unwashed football socks, mouldy mushrooms and damp cardboard. At its worst, a corked wine is completely undrinkable. But if the taint is only slight – just enough to mute the true flavours of the wine – you may conclude that the wine is simply not to your liking and will never buy it again.

Oxidized wine

When a wine reeks of sherry, appears slightly murky in appearance and is yellow-brown in colour, it means that it has absorbed excess oxygen, that is, it is oxidized and is fast becoming vinegar. This happens when air attacks wine, usually because the cork has dried out, which is why bottles stoppered with a natural cork should be stored on their sides.

Tartrate crystals

If you spot something that looks like sugar or shards of glass clinging to your glass, or to the cork, then do not worry. These are natural deposits formed by the precipitation of tartaric acid and are odourless, tasteless and perfectly harmless.

Flavour trails

There are a number of paths to explore if you want to try something different without taking too much of a risk.

Follow those taste triggers

Next time you take a slurp of your favourite wine, think about its smell and taste. What makes it so pleasurable? Does the aroma remind you of a favourite flower? Perhaps it tastes of a fruit of which you are fond. Remember, these primary scents and flavours come from the grape. So once you have identified the variety, you will probably enjoy other wines made from it.

Kick off your taste trigger trail by drinking wines created from the same grape in the same country. If, say, your ideal wine is a Sauvignon Blanc from New Zealand's Marlborough region, choose a Sauvignon made by another Marlborough producer, or one that hails from an alternative Kiwi region.

Take the next step

To stick with our model, now buy a Sauvignon from another country and then move on to other regions within that country. To advance further, experiment with a Sauvignon/Semillon blend – which may then lead you to investigate wines made solely from the Semillon grape.

Trading up

Another 'safe' approach is to work out if your favourite fits into any classification system. If you are keen on simple Chianti, for instance, upgrade to Chianti Riserva. You will experience the same kind of flavours, but they will be more intense.

Other sources
- Organize a wine tasting party with friends, or join a local wine society.
- Consult a wine merchant for further advice about creating your own flavour trails.
- Check the Amazon website for DVDs on wine. Do not waste your money on old editions, however – the world of wine is changing all the time!
- Check the internet and your local media for information about wine courses in your area.

Weblinks
- For information on the quality of individual vintages, visit: www.winemag.com www.bbr.com www.decanter.com

3 White wines

Some people find red wines really hard to drink, but there are few who do not sing the praises of a decent glass of white. It is easy to see why, because it slips down the throat easily and is highly versatile, being quaffable with or without food. While this chapter divides these wines into four main styles, bear in mind that the edges can become a little blurred – for example, nine times out of ten, tangy whites are also highly aromatic. Sweet white wines are treated separately later on in their own chapter.

How white wines are made

Broadly speaking – and setting aside the enormous influence of the grape variety – the overall style and flavour of any dry white is determined by the type of fermentation vessel, the temperature at which the fermentation takes place and whether or not the wine receives any ageing in the winery.

A white wine glass should always be tulip-shaped, because the narrowing neck helps to trap, funnel and magnify aromas.

Pre-fermentation

No colour is required for white wines, of course, so the juice is separated from the grape skins as soon as they are pressed.

Air is excluded as far as possible throughout the whole winemaking procedure, though if the juice is destined to become premium wine, it is exposed to a small amount of oxygen prior to fermentation if the producer thinks it will benefit the finished wine.

Simple, easy-drinking styles

These are fermented in stainless steel vats or concrete tanks lined with epoxy resin. Temperature control is critical – simple white wines retain their fruity aromas and flavours only as long as fermentation temperatures are maintained between 12 °C/54 °F and 20 °C/68 °F.

Premium wines

Frequently, these styles are fermented in small oak barrels, and at higher temperatures, in order to add extra layers of flavour. This is further encouraged by stirring the lees (the yeasty sediment) from time to time. When fermentation is complete, the wine is transferred to new barrels for around six to eight months during which time the wine develops extra flavour.

Practical matters

Even the most expensive dry white wine will not taste good if you open it either before or after it has reached its peak. In order to enjoy it at its best, it also pays to drink it at the correct temperature, though this varies from wine to wine.

When to drink them

The vast majority of dry whites are made specifically for early drinking. In practice, this means they should be drunk within six months to a year of leaving the winery, but as there is no certainty of knowing when this occurred, always buy the most recent vintage available.

Exceptions to this are mid-priced, dry whites from Alsace, Jurançon, the Loire and the New World, which will keep for between three and five years, and top class dry whites from Bordeaux, Burgundy, the Loire, the Rhône and Australian Rieslings and Semillons, which have in-built longevity and can be drunk at five to ten years old.

watch out!

Avoid over-chilling
If a wine is served too cold, much of its taste – and, more importantly, most of its aroma – will be masked.

Ideal serving temperatures

Style	Example	Temperature
Neutral	Frascati (Italy)	4°-6°C/ 39°-43°F
Tangy	New Zealand Sauvignon Blanc	6°-8°C/ 43°-46°F
Aromatic	Gewürztraminer (from anywhere)	8°-10°C/ 46°-50°F
Buttery	Australian Oaked Chardonnay	8°-10°C/ 46°-50°F

Aromatic whites

Not to put too fine a point on it, these are the kind of wines that grab you by the nostrils! Their heady perfume jumps from the glass and it is no exaggeration to say that you can often smell these wines long before your nose is anywhere near them. However, the promise of the bouquet is always followed by a host of thrilling flavours.

must know

Top ten producers
▶ Brown Brothers (Muscat; Australia)
▶ Chapel Hill (Irsai Olivér; Hungary)
▶ Cuilleron (Condrieu; France)
▶ Etchart (Torrontés; Argentina)
▶ Fetzer (Viognier; California)
▶ Jordan (Chenin Blanc; South Africa)
▶ Rolly Gassmann (Muscat; France)
▶ Pazo de Señoras (Albariño; Spain)
▶ Yalumba (Viognier; Australia)
▶ Zind Humbrecht (Gewürztraminer; France)

Delicate, highly scented styles

An arresting perfume of rose petals, grapes and musk, a very pale colour and a certain fragility of character is the signature of these wines. To taste, you can anticipate lively, crisp flavours of a fresh fruit salad crammed with hothouse grapes and chunks of mango and peach, all rounded off by a hint of spice and a snap of lemon-lime acidity.

Typical countries, typical grapes

One might assume that highly-delicate wines can be produced only in Old World countries with cool climates and it is true that the majority of them are made in such places. France, for instance, is the principal source of wine created from the Muscat grape, which is one of the finest exponents of this style. But terrific Muscat is also made in Australia, albeit in a more mouth-filling style, which proves that this kind of wine can be created in the New World as long as the vines are planted at high altitudes (where temperatures are much lower).

Other grape names to look for are Torrontés (an Argentinian speciality that also bears out the high altitude theory) and Irsai Olivér, Hárslevelü and Leányka, varieties indigenous to Hungary.

Names to look for

Most wines of this style are labelled by grape variety (even in the Old World), which makes them very easy to find on the shelves! For the best examples, however, try to find wines that carry the name of the following top regions:

- Alsace (France) for Muscat
- Balatonboglar (Hungary) for Irsai Olivér and Hárslevelü
- Cafayate (Argentina) for Torrontés
- Victoria (Australia) for Muscat
- Vin de Pays d'Oc (France) for Muscat

Fruity, floral styles

Once again, the exact nature of these wines depends on climate and, as a rule, the cooler it is, the fresher and more delicate the wine will be. Nonetheless, every wine of this style is hauntingly fragrant and generously fruity. Expect a bouquet of spring flowers, May-blossom, honeysuckle, pot-pourri, pink grapefruit and, sometimes, whispers of fennel and camomile. In taste, anticipate heavenly flavours of fresh apricots, pear, citrus fruits, overripe white peach and, occasionally, an allusion of nutmeg and cinnamon, all underpinned by a mouth-tingling, grapefruity acidity. Riper styles from warmer areas also embrace hints of pineapple, passion fruit, mango and honeydew melon.

Vines planted at higher altitudes yield grapes that produce fresher, more delicate white wines.

Typical countries, typical grapes

Viognier is the archetypal grape of this style and the finest wines are made in France's Rhône Valley, South Australia's Eden Valley, California's

You can really smell these wines - and the stronger the bouquet, the stronger the taste!

You will generally find that the name of the grape gives a better indication of wine style than the name of the vineyard it came from.

Mendocino, Sonoma and Santa Barbara regions and South Africa's Paarl region. Italy's northeastern, alpine Trentino-Alto Adige and Friuli-Venezia Giulia regions are also renowned for mountain fresh, elegant, dry whites that are always beautifully floral and fruity, almost regardless of the grape from which they are made. Over in Spain, the Albariño grape is responsible for this style, though the wines it makes are slightly herbier than the norm. In Germany and Austria, Scheurebe can be good, whilst England makes its mark with Schönburger.

Names to look for

For New World versions, you need only look for the name of the grape varieties from the relevant countries and regions mentioned above. In the Old World, modern, southern French wines are increasingly being labelled by grape variety, as are those of Italy's Friuli-Venezia Giulia and Trentino-Alto Adige regions, all German and Austrian Scheurebe and English Schönburger, so they are quite easy to find.

Pungent styles

This unique style enjoys unmistakable and extremely powerful aromas of lychees, tea roses and sweet peas. The lychee character follows through to the palate, alongside flavours of other exotic fruits, honeydew melon, Turkish Delight and a scraping of freshly-grated ginger root.

Typical countries, typical grapes

One grape only provides this highly-individual style and that is Gewürztraminer. The finest and most pungent hail from France's Alsace region, though excellent, slightly lighter-bodied examples are also made in Northern Italy, Germany, Hungary, New Zealand and California (especially from Mendocino County).

Names to look for

While this style is always labelled by grape variety, even in France, it is always wise to read the back label to check that the wine is dry to taste; you don't want any nasty surprises.

Gewürztraminer wines can be sweet, so read the label carefully if you are looking for a dry white wine.

Aromatic whites with food

Aromatic whites lend themselves particularly well to the fragrant and spicy cuisines associated with the Far East, though they are also the perfect accompaniment to many conventional Western dishes. As a rule, the more distinctive the flavour of the food, the more spicy and floral the wine should be.

watch out!

White wine enemies
Artichoke, spinach, raw onion, vinegar, salted peanuts, Habanero and Thai bird's eye chillies.

Starters and snacks

Talking of strong flavours, Gewürztraminer is wonderful with chicken liver pâté, and with both French onion and butternut squash soups. And talking of soup, carrot and coriander soup is better with a gentler wine such as Muscat or Torrontés, while Riesling is delicious with celery soup. Interestingly, both Gewürztraminer and Riesling work well with grilled Thai-style prawns, but only the latter is suitable for the humbler prawn cocktail. Riesling also goes well with corn on the cob and smoked trout.

Münster cheese and Gewürztraminer make a very pleasing combination.

Main courses

If you are eating dishes containing crab, hake or halibut, Albariño is the wine of choice. For roast goose and coronation chicken, try Gewürztraminer, and looking to the Far East again, this is also excellent with hot chicken curries, vegetable balti and beef in black bean sauce. For milder fare, such as chicken with cashew nuts, Peking duck, chicken korma and chicken with lime and coriander, choose Riesling. Viognier is also great with many main course dishes, including honey-glazed duck, grilled salmon and chicken satay.

Hamburg

□ BERLIN

Hannover

Düsseldorf

MITTELRHEIN

AHR
Bonn

RHEINGAU

MOSEL-SAAR-RUWER

Frankfurt am Main

NAHE

Trier

FRANKEN

RHEINHESSEN

BADEN

PFALZ

BADEN

WÜRTTEMBERG

Stuttgart

Danube (Donau)

BADEN

Munich (München)

BADEN

Elbe

Havel

Spree

Saale

Ems

Hunte

Weser

Rhein

German wine regions

About 80 per cent of Germany's vineyards are planted with white grapes. This is because the country is at the northerly limit of viticulture and therefore possesses a harsh climate that many red varieties cannot tolerate. Most of the vineyards are concentrated in the warmer southwest corner of the country and are located on the sunnier south-facing slopes, almost always close to a river. The mists that rise from these rivers during the autumn months help to protect grapes from early frost.

Tangy whites

Virtually all tangy whites are also extremely aromatic. The chief difference between the two styles lies in their acidity – tangy whites are always assertive, bracing, penetrating, biting, zingy and mouthwatering, thanks to long growing seasons in cool climates which slowly draw out aromas and flavours to optimum effect.

watch out!

Chilean Sauvignon Blanc
Always buy Chilean Sauvignon Blanc from a reputable producer because many so-called Sauvignons are in reality made from the inferior Sauvignonasse grape. Whilst it offers many of the same aromas and flavours, they fade to nothing extremely quickly.

New Zealand has the perfect climate for the production of grapes that produce tangy dry whites.

Intense, grassy styles

Take a deep breath. The spectrum of dazzling, exhilarating and explosive aromas and flavours of these spiky, bone-dry, often deeply herbaceous wines takes in gooseberries, asparagus, nettles, passion fruit, crushed tomato leaf, elderflower, Granny Smith apples, flowering currant, kiwi fruit, freshly-sliced green capsicum, newly-mown lawns, grapefruit, lime cordial and (it really must be said!), sweaty armpits and cat's pee. And, as unbelievable as it may sound, there may even be a puff of smoke and a suggestion of wet stone – pick up a pebble next time it rains, or when you are passing a stream, to see what I mean! Not every wine will exhibit all of these aromas and flavours, but you will notice a fair whack of them each time you open a bottle of this style.

Typical countries, typical grapes

New Zealand Sauvignon Blanc is the ultimate definition of this vivacious, tight-knit style, most especially in the Marlborough region of South Island. Admirable alternatives include wines created from the same grape in South Africa (the best from the regions of Constantia, Elgin and Robertson), France's Loire Valley, Austria (where Styria is the top spot) and, every now and then, Hungary. Also, wines made from Arinto in Portugal, Assyrtiko in Greece and Bacchus and Huxelrebe in England can give a similar bouquet and taste, though they are not in the same class with regard to quality.

Names to look for

It is painless to find wines of this style from the New World, Austria, Hungary and England because they are always labelled by grape variety. In France, however, you are forced to be more canny, in that you must know where these wines are made and are therefore obliged to look for the name of the appellation. Here are the best of them, all from the Loire Valley:

- ▶ Menetou-Salon
- ▶ Pouilly-Fumé
- ▶ Quincy
- ▶ Reuilly
- ▶ Sancerre
- ▶ Sauvignon de Touraine

Softer styles

These quaffable wines display many of the squeaky clean smells and tastes of their more extrovert and concentrated, tangy cousins,

The Loire region in France is home to some of the world's most famous white wine vineyards.

though in a more restrained and relaxed manner because the grapes are grown in warmer areas. Riper fruit flavours creep in, such as pineapple, peach, honeydew melon, pear, greengages and figs.

Typical countries, typical grapes
Once more it is the Sauvignon Blanc grape variety that throws up this style, this time in Argentina, Chile, California, Spain and Italy and, again, in certain parts of France. In addition, wines made from Colombard grapes grown in South Africa and southern France, and from Verdelho in Australia, also create wines with these flavours.

Names to look for
New World and Italian versions all state the name of the grape variety on the label. When it comes to European versions, however, you need to track down the following (all made from Sauvignon Blanc):

▶ Bergerac (southwest France)
▶ Côtes de Duras (southwest France)
▶ Entre-Deux-Mers (Bordeaux, France)
▶ Graves (Bordeaux, France)
▶ Inexpensive Bordeaux Blanc (France)
▶ Pessac-Léognan (Bordeaux, France)
▶ Rueda (Castilla-y-León, Spain)

Minerally styles
These wines express all the brio of tangy whites in the form of zippy orchard fruit, the juice of waxy limes, yellow plums, satsumas and a lavish boost of zesty grapefruit. What sets this style apart, however, is an austere, steely, flinty core and a wonderful aroma of apple-blossom, hay and, when given a little ageing, an inviting whiff of honey, lanolin, smoke and, very often, even an intimation of kerosene.

Typical countries, typical grapes

Riesling is the grape variety to look for if you enjoy this style of wine and the finest wines in this bracket hail from Germany, Austria and northern France in the Old World, and Australia, New Zealand, New York State, Oregon and Canada in the New World.

Names to look for

Generally speaking, the weightiest, most potent wines of this style are Rieslings made in France's Alsace region. For the leanest, freshest styles, choose from the following regions and appellations:

▶ Baden, Mosel-Saar-Ruwer and Nahe (Germany)
▶ Clare Valley, Coonawarra, Eden Valley and Tasmania (Australia)
▶ Finger Lakes and Washington State (USA)
▶ Marlborough and Nelson (New Zealand)
▶ Niagara Peninsula (Ontario, Canada)
▶ Wachau (Austria) for Riesling

An appreciation of the names and characteristics of different wine regions will assist you in selecting wines and creating a cellar.

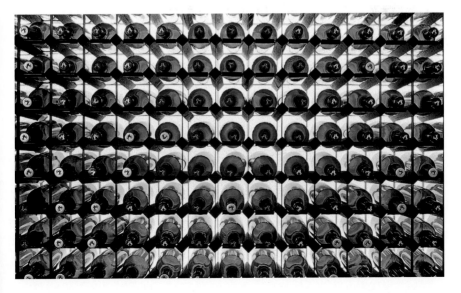

Tangy whites with food

Tangy whites can be drunk alongside a wide variety of dishes. Some foods, however, call for the bold, upfront flavours found in many New World versions, whilst others go better with the more restrained styles of the Old World. They are also a terrific complement to many seafood and fish dishes.

New Zealand green lipped mussels and New Zealand Sauvignon Blanc are perfect partners.

Starters and snacks

Let us start with the dishes with which any tangy white will work: asparagus soup, French onion soup, tomato soup, gazpacho, seafood chowder, asparagus with hollandaise sauce, mussels, grilled prawns, whitebait, crab, Caesar salad, warm bacon and avocado salad, avocado with prawns and goat's cheese tart. For more subtle matches, choose Bordeaux Blanc or Vin de Pays des Côtes de Gascogne for mushroom soup, New Zealand Sauvignon Blanc for bean salad, taramasalata and gravadlax, and Loire Sauvignon Blanc for smoked trout.

Main courses

New World tangy whites are tremendous when drunk alongside Thai beef salad, pasta in pesto sauce, swordfish steaks, chicken Kiev, langoustines and Cajun cuisine. Partner Old World wines with southern fried chicken, halibut, turbot, sea bass, sole, red mullet and roast pork. Pretty much any tangy white is a perfect match with Thai green curry, fish pie, chicken with lime and coriander, tandoori chicken, fish and chips, kedgeree, squid and cheese fondue.

New Zealand wine regions

New Zealand may be a small country, but it spans 1,600km north to south, which would stretch from Bordeaux to Morocco if transposed to European latitudes. The variation in mesoclimates and terrain therefore has a considerable impact on wine style. Nevertheless, every vine enjoys plenty of sunshine and a long, slow ripening period helps to retain the vibrant flavours that make New Zealand wines so distinctive. Seven times more white varieties are planted than red, but there is a growing emphasis on red wine production, driven by demand.

3 White wines

Flavour trails

Style	Country	Principal source(s)	Principal grape(s)
Aromatic, delicate, highly scented	Argentina	Cafayate	Torrontés
	Australia	Victoria	Muscat
	France	Alsace; Vin de Pays d'Oc	Muscat
	Hungary	Balatonboglar	Irsai Olivér; Hárslevelü; Leányka
Aromatic, fruity, floral	Australia	South Australia	Viognier
	Austria	Wachau	Scheurebe
	England	South	Schönburger
	France	Rhône	Viognier
	Germany	Everywhere	Scheurebe
	South Africa	Paarl	Viognier
	Spain	Galicia	Albariño
	USA	California	Viognier
Aromatic, pungent	France	Alsace	Gewürztraminer
	Germany	Baden; Pfalz; Sachsen; Württemberg	Gewürztraminer
	Hungary	Villány-Siklós	Gewürztraminer
	Italy	Friuli-Venezia Giulia; Trentino-Alto Adige	Gewürztraminer
	New Zealand	Martinborough	Gewürztraminer
	USA	California	Gewürztraminer
Neutral, crisp, nervy	Argentina	Mendoza	Chardonnay (unoaked)
	Chile	Cachapoal; Casablanca; Curicó	Chardonnay (unoaked)
	France	Burgundy; Loire; Vin de Pays d'Oc	Aligoté; Chardonnay (unoaked); Melon de Bourgogne
	Italy	Friuli-Venezia Giulia; Trentino-Alto Adige	Chardonnay (unoaked); Vermentino; Vernaccia
	New Zealand	Everywhere	Chardonnay (unoaked)
	Portugal	Vinho Verde	Alvarinho/Arinto/

Flavour trails

Style	Country	Principal source(s)	Principal grape(s)
			Escagna Cão / Loureiro/ Trajadura blend
	South Africa	Everywhere	Chardonnay (unoaked)
	Switzerland	Geneva; Valais; Vaud	Chasselas
Neutral, fruity	Argentina	Mendoza	Chenin Blanc (unoaked)
	Austria	Styria; Wachau	Grüner Veltliner; Pinot Blanc; Pinot Gris
	Bulgaria	Black Sea	Chardonnay (unoaked); Pinot Blanc
	Canada	Niagara Peninsula; Okanagan Valley	Pinot Gris
	France	Alsace; Loire	Chenin Blanc (unoaked); Pinot Blanc; Pinot Gris
	Germany	Baden; Pfalz	Grauburgunder
	Hungary	Eger; Skekszárd; Siklós	Chardonnay (unoaked); Pinot Blanc
	Italy	Friuli-Venezia Giulia; Sicily; Trentino-Alto Adige; Tuscany	Chardonnay (unoaked); Pinot Blanc; Pinot Grigio
	New Zealand	Central Otago	Pinot Gris
	South Africa	Everywhere	Chenin Blanc (unoaked)
	USA	Oregon	Pinot Gris
Neutral, nutty-edged	Italy	Campania; Emilia-Romagna; Lazio; Lombardia; Marche; Piemonte; Puglia; Umbria; Tuscany; Veneto	Various, mainly Trebbiano-based indigenous blends
Richer, bolder, big, sunshine-ripe	Australia	Hunter Valley; Goulburn Valley	Chardonnay (oaked); Marsanne
	Spain	Costers del Segre	Chardonnay (oaked)
	USA	California	Chardonnay (oaked)

3 White wines

Flavour trails

Style	Country	Principal source(s)	Principal grape(s)
Richer, bolder, elegant, sophisticated	Australia	Adelaide Hills; Margaret River; Tasmania; Yarra Valley	Chardonnay (oaked)
	Canada	Niagara Peninsula; Okanagan Valley	Chardonnay (oaked)
	France	Burgundy	Chardonnay (oaked)
	New Zealand	Canterbury; Marlborough; Nelson	Chardonnay (oaked)
	South Africa	Robertson; Stellenbosch; Walker Bay	Chardonnay (oaked)
	Spain	Navarra; Somontano	Chardonnay (oaked)
	USA	New York State; Oregon; Washington State	Chardonnay (oaked)
Richer, bolder, fruitier	Australia	Barossa Valley; Clare Valley; Hunter Valley; Margaret River	Sauvignon Blanc/Sémillon blend; Semillon
	France	Bordeaux; Loire	Chenin Blanc (oaked); Sauvignon Blanc/Sémillon blend
	New Zealand	North Island	Sauvignon Blanc (oaked)
	South Africa	Paarl	Chenin Blanc (oaked)
	Spain	Rioja	Macabeo/Garnacha Blanco/Malvasia blend
	USA	California	Chenin Blanc (oaked); Sauvignon Blanc (oaked)
Tangy, intense, grassy	Austria	Styria	Sauvignon Blanc
	England	South	Bacchus; Huxelrebe
	France	Loire	Sauvignon Blanc
	Greece	Santorini	Assyrtiko
	Hungary	Mátraalja; Mór	Sauvignon Blanc
	New Zealand	Marlborough	Sauvignon Blanc
	Portugal	Central; south	Arinto
	South Africa	Constantia; Elgin; Robertson	Sauvignon Blanc

Flavour trails

Style	Country	Principal source(s)	Principal grape(s)
Tangy, minerally	Australia	Clare Valley; Coonawarra; Eden Valley; Tasmania	Riesling
	Austria	Wachau	Riesling
	Canada	Niagara Peninsula	Riesling
	France	Alsace; Loire	Chenin Blanc (unoaked); Riesling
	Germany	Baden; Pfalz; Mosel-Saar-Ruwer; Nahe; Rheingau; Rheinhessen	Riesling
	New Zealand	Marlborough; Nelson	Riesling
	USA	New York State; Oregon; Washington State	Riesling
Tangy, softer	Argentina	Mendoza	Sauvignon Blanc
	Australia	Victoria	Verdelho
	Chile	Casablanca Valley	Sauvignon Blanc
	France	Bergerac; Bordeaux; Loire; southwest	Colombard; Sauvignon Blanc
	Italy	Friuli-Venezia Giulia; Trentino-Alto Adige	Sauvignon Blanc
	South Africa	Everywhere	Colombard
	Spain	Castilla-y-León	Sauvignon Blanc
	USA	California	Sauvignon Blanc

Richer, bolder whites

These range from the restrained yet powerful, to the big and blowsy. Almost invariably – and 'almost' is important to say, because exceptions do exist – they are fermented and/or aged in oak and, as we know from the previous chapters, it is the oak that adds those extra dimensions of flavour and complexity.

Elegant, sophisticated styles

These exquisite, opulent and sophisticated wines offer oatmealy, creamy tones and sublime pear, nectarines, honey, quince, figs, cashew nuts, hazelnuts, melted butter and mineral tastes, all cut by a balancing splash of lemon acidity. On paper, this may sound as if this style boasts masses of flavour, but in reality they are wonderfully subtle, well-poised and finely-balanced wines of great finesse.

Chardonnay grapes are among the most widely used in the world of white wine. They offer both tremendous versatility and consistently popular flavours.

Typical countries, typical grapes

These flavours are unique to barrel-fermented and/or barrel-aged Chardonnay and there are precious few wine-producing countries that do not make this kind of wine. It takes much skill and a thorough understanding of the application of oak to achieve the very best wines, however, and it is also true to say that top wines can only really be made successfully in cool climates. For this reason, the finest examples come from France, Canada, New Zealand and the cooler areas of Spain, Australia, South Africa and the United States.

Names to look for

Burgundy has been the spiritual home of this style of dry white wine for centuries, a style that everyone wishes to emulate. Mind you, it is extremely unlikely that you will find the word Chardonnay on the label! Here, these classic wines are named after the village in which the grapes were grown, or in the case of the Grands Crus (premium, world-beating wines that reach dizzying heights of quality, grace, longevity ... and price!), after the vineyard. The New World is more accommodating, however, so you need only look for Chardonnay and an indication that it has been barrel-fermented and/or aged. For the finest wines, choose from the following regions or appellations:

It is not only the ancient vineyards of Burgundy that produce white wines of the highest standard. The New World offers many superb whites.

► Adelaide Hills (South Australia)
► Bâtard-Montrachet (Grand Cru vineyard, Burgundy, France)
► Canterbury (New Zealand)
► Chassagne-Montrachet (Grand Cru vineyard, Burgundy, France)
► Corton-Charlemagne (Grand Cru vineyard, Burgundy, France)
► Long Island (New York State, USA)
► Margaret River (Western Australia)
► Marlborough (New Zealand)
► Meursault (Burgundy, France)
► Montrachet (Grand Cru vineyard, Burgundy, France)
► Navarra (Spain)
► Nelson (New Zealand)
► Niagara Peninsula (Ontario, Canada)
► Pipers Brook (Tasmania, Australia)
► Pouilly-Fuissé (Burgundy, France)
► Pouilly-Vinzelles (Burgundy, France)
► Puligny-Montrachet (Burgundy, France)
► Robertson (South Africa)
► Rully (Burgundy, France)
► Saint-Véran (Burgundy, France)
► Somontano (Spain)
► Stellenbosch (South Africa)
► Viré-Clessé (Burgundy, France)
► Walker Bay (South Africa)
► Washington State (USA)
► Yarra Valley (Victoria, Australia)

Kangaroos are a regular feature in Australian vineyards but they are considered a pest because they like to eat the grapes!

Fruitier styles

There are two broad categories within this particular style. Firstly, there are wines with textures that can be described as waxy, custardy, creamy, lush, fleshy, lanolin-soft and well-rounded. These wines enjoy flavours of honey, nectarine, tinned pineapple, apricot, peach, nuts, chunky orange marmalade spread thickly on buttered toast and slices of lemon and lime. Note that not all wines of this style have been in contact with oak!

The second group within this style comprises mature, barrel-aged wines that have developed aromas of hay, beeswax and wet wool, and vibrant flavours of apples, almonds, melon, fig, pear, guava, banana, pear, pineapple and hot toast dripping with butter and honey.

Typical countries, typical grapes

Many of the wines that fall into the first group are blends of grape varieties. For example, traditional French whites from Bordeaux are made from a mix of Sauvignon Blanc and Sémillon. Some Australian Semillons – oaked or unoaked – also share these characteristics, as well as oaked Sauvignon Blanc from New Zealand and California. Mature, barrel-fermented Chenin Blanc from France, South Africa and California are typical of the second group of flavours.

Names to look for

Specific names to track down are:
▶ Barossa Valley (South Australia) for oaked Semillon
▶ Graves (Bordeaux, France) for Sauvignon Blanc/Sémillon blends

- Hunter Valley (New South Wales, Australia) for mature, unoaked Semillon
- Pessac-Léognan (Bordeaux, France) for Sauvignon Blanc/Sémillon blends

Big, sunshine-ripe styles

If you want a sumptuous, lush, fruit-driven wine, then you must choose an oak-aged wine made from grapes grown in sunny and hot climes where they ripen to perfection. These golden-coloured, syrupy-smooth whites are always big and fat, blowsy and full-bodied, flaunting the taste of ripe tropical fruits, caramelized bananas, butterscotch and rich honey.

Typical countries, typical grapes

It will come as no surprise that these wines are produced mainly in the New World, especially in Australia and California, though they also emanate from Spain. These golden-coloured, syrupy-smooth whites are always big and fat, blowsy and full-bodied, flaunting the taste of ripe tropical fruits, caramelized bananas, butterscotch and rich honey. Most are created from Chardonnay or Marsanne grapes.

Names to look for

Try these well-respected names:
- Alexander Valley (California, USA) for Chardonnay
- Carneros (California, USA) for Chardonnay
- Costers del Segre (Spain) for Chardonnay
- Goulburn Valley (Victoria, Australia) for Marsanne
- Hunter Valley (New South Wales, Australia) for Chardonnay
- Monterey County (California, USA) for Chardonnay

It takes a delicate hand to ensure that oak complements the flavour of a wine without spoiling it.

Richer, bolder whites with food

By definition, buttery whites from anywhere around the world are complex and full-bodied in style and are therefore able to cope with dishes that boast a more robust nature, most especially those that rely on the powerful flavours presented by richly-flavoured fish and the kind of sauces with which they are eaten.

The flavours of king prawns are perfectly complemented by a good, rich Meursault.

Starters and snacks

Everyday oaked Chardonnay is ideal with tomato and mozzarella salad, potted shrimps and many other seafood-based starters. Its relatively straightforward style works with any number of different flavours.

Reserve top white Burgundies for smoked salmon, smoked trout pâté, gravadlax, Coquilles St Jacques, scallops mornay and lobster bisque.

Main courses

Chargrilled chicken with herbs, macaroni cheese, monkfish, fresh mackerel, roast turkey, roast chicken, roast pork, quiche, chicken tikka masala, Tex-Mex, barbecued fish, paella, Thai curries ... these everyday dishes need only be matched by everyday oaked Chardonnay. But lobster thermidor, rabbit in mustard sauce, sole (both Dover and lemon) and meaty, fleshy fish such as Atlantic salmon cutlets, chargrilled tuna and swordfish steaks demand to be complemented by a good white Burgundy. Indeed, save your expensive white Burgundies for dinner parties and other special occasions when you are likely to be using recipes that require expensive ingredients.

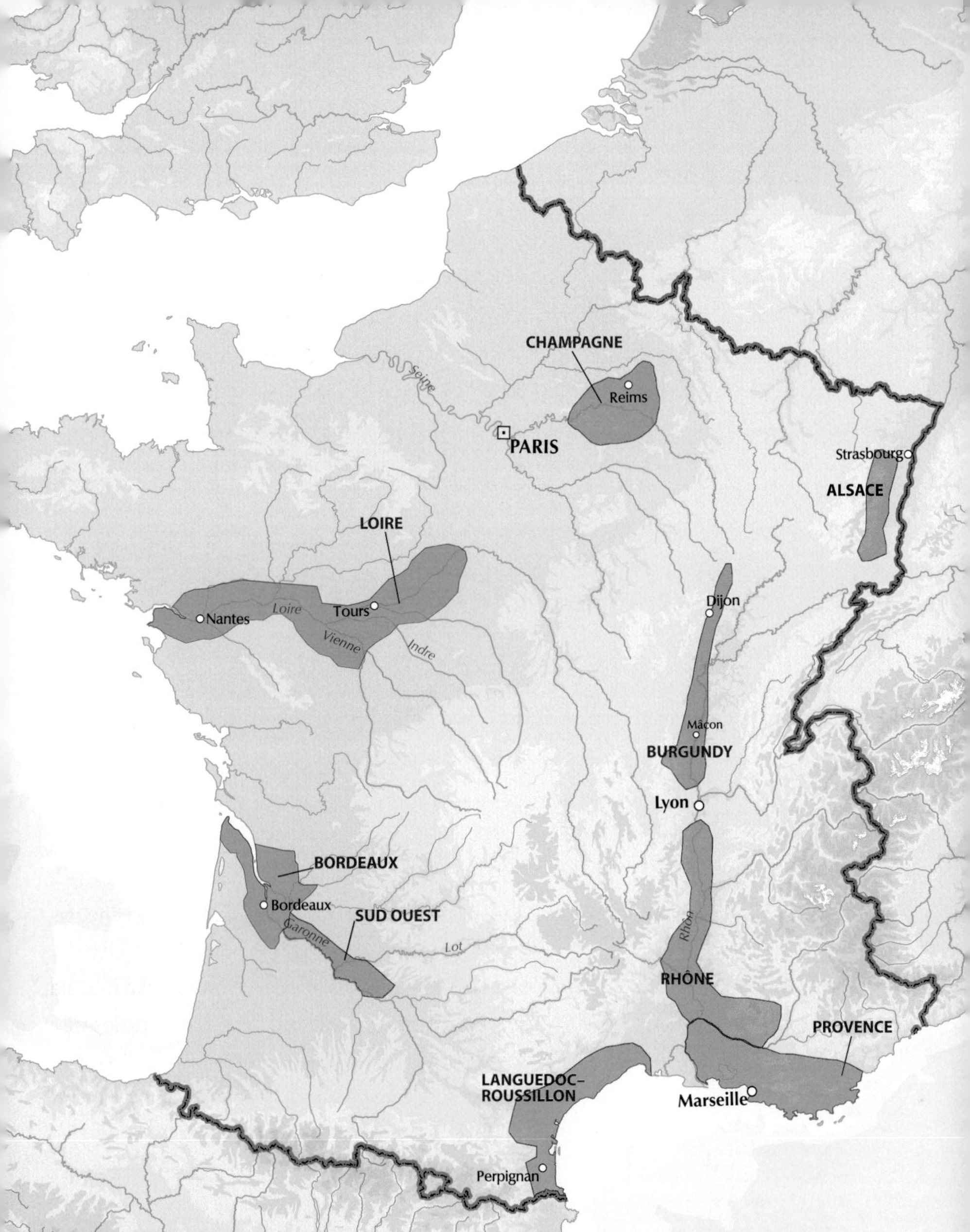

CHAMPAGNE

Reims

PARIS

Strasbourg

ALSACE

LOIRE

Seine

Dijon

Nantes

Loire

Tours

Vienne

Indre

Mâcon

BURGUNDY

Lyon

BORDEAUX

Bordeaux

SUD OUEST

Garonne

Lot

Rhône

RHÔNE

PROVENCE

LANGUEDOC-
ROUSSILLON

Marseille

Perpignan

French wine regions

France is the world's largest wine producer and every style of wine is made under a rigid appellation system that has done much to protect many grape varieties that would have otherwise long disappeared. More red and rosé is made than white, the majority hailing from the warmer, southern half of the country. France remains the model for the rest of the world's winemakers, who aspire to replicate her top quality wines.

Neutral whites

In contrast to other white wines, neutral dry whites are relatively subdued. There is no upfront fruit here – think stony kernels rather than moist skins and soft flesh. But this is not to say that neutral equals dull – far from it! These wines may be undemanding, but they can be extremely flavoursome and attractive.

Casablanca Valley in Chile is the home of many vineyards producing fine, dry, neutrally flavoured white wines.

Crisp, nervy styles

These wines are usually watery or greeny-gold in colour and are always light-bodied. They possess a refreshing, lively acidity – which may even be rasping at times – because they are made in cool regions where the grapes ripen over a long period, which helps to concentrate their aroma and taste. If oak is exploited in the production of these styles – which is rare – it is used very cautiously.

Bone dry yet well-rounded to taste, they embrace very pure flavours of lemons, crunchy green apples, melon, quince, greengages, tangerines and peach skin, though some wines flaunt delicate notes of tropical fruit, grapefruit peel, bay leaves and, possibly, a surprisingly appealing iodine twang.

Typical countries, typical grapes

Unoaked Chardonnay grown in cool climates provides the perfect example of this kind of wine – lean and taut, with a steely, minerally texture, it seems to absorb the individual character of the region in which it is grown. The best come from New Zealand, Argentina, Chile (especially the Cachapoal, Casablanca and Curicó regions), South

Africa, southern France and Italy's Trentino-Alto Adige and Friuli-Venezia Giulia regions.

France is also home to the Melon de Bourgogne grape, which is responsible for Muscadet, one of the most famous and popular wines from the Loire Valley, and to the Aligoté grape, a speciality of Burgundy. Other good examples of this style are made in Portugal (from a blend of Alvarinho, Arinto, Escagna Cão, Loureiro and Trajadura), Switzerland (from Chasselas) and in Italy (from Vermentino and Vernaccia).

The Vinho Verde region of northwest Portugal.

Names to look for

The key words to look for on New World bottles are 'unoaked', 'cool climate' and 'Chardonnay'. In the Old World, you should buy these particular names:

▶ Chablis (Burgundy, France)
▶ Chardonnay, Vin de Pays d'Oc (southern France)
▶ Muscadet de Sèvre-et-Maine Sur Lie (Loire Valley, France)
▶ Muscadet des Coteaux de la Loire (Loire Valley, France)
▶ Muscadet Côtes de Grand-Lieu (Loire Valley, France)
▶ Vinho Verde (northwest Portugal)

Nutty-edged styles

While these wines are always bone dry, they also share a striking taste of crushed almonds and sour cream. Sometimes there may be a streak of citrus fruit or hints of ripe apple, goldengage or peach, and, occasionally, faint traces of green leaves and brown earth. You may also detect a

Countless different varieties of white grapes have been grown throughout the Old World of wine for centuries.

Local winemaking laws

One important factor that has not been mentioned so far is that the grape varieties used to create quality Old World wines are strictly governed by the rules of each appellation, determined by hundreds of years of evidence of what grows best where. In Italy, for example, Frascati can only be made from a blend of Malvasia and Trebbiano grapes under the specific *Denominazione di Origine Controllata* (DOC) rules for Frascati. If producers use different grapes, then the wine cannot be called Frascati and must be declassified to Vino da Tavola.

---

sprinkling of cinnamon, camomile, thyme and fennel, or a twist of liquorice.

Typical countries, typical grapes

This style of wine is an Italian speciality and you will rarely find them in other Old World countries, never mind the New World. They are made from blends of indigenous grapes whose names rarely appear on labels, so you need not worry about searching for specific varieties. Instead, you should be looking for specific appellations.

Names to look for

The overall quality of these wines has improved greatly of late. The most popular and reliable names include:

▶ Albana di Romagna (Emilia-Romagna)
▶ Bianco di Custoza (Veneto)
▶ Est! Est!! Est!!! (Lazio)
▶ Falerno del Massico (Campania)
▶ Frascati (Lazio)
▶ Gavi (Piemonte)
▶ Lacryma Christi del Vesuvio (Campania)
▶ Lugana (Lombardia)
▶ Martina Franca (Puglia)
▶ Orvieto (Umbria)
▶ Soave (Veneto)
▶ Verdicchio dei Castelli di Jesi (Marche)

Fruitier styles

While these easy-drinking wines fundamentally remain fresh and neutral in personality, their flavours are slightly more intense and complex in character and they can feel weightier in the mouth. Here you will find succulent flavours of greengage, melon, pear, lemon, lime, orange, peach and apple, alongside touches of angelica, white pepper, celery, honey, marzipan and butterscotch, traces of cake spice and, maybe, some smoky notes.

Typical countries, typical grapes

This style of wine crops up everywhere in the world and they are often made from blends of grapes (Colombard/Chenin Blanc, for example). The most interesting, however, are varietal wines made from Pinot Grigio.

Names to look for

- Alsace (France) for Pinot Gris
- Central Otago (New Zealand) for Pinot Gris
- Friuli-Venezia Giulia (Italy) for Pinot Blanc and Pinot Gris
- Sicily (France) for Chardonnay
- Styria (Austria) for Chardonnay
- Tuscany (Italy) for Chardonnay
- Wachau (Austria) for Grüner Veltliner

Neutral dry whites are incredibly easy to drink at any time, with or without food.

Neutral whites with food

If faced with the dilemma of not knowing which wine to serve with what, you can be assured that a neutral white will almost always fit the bill. As this style of wine is made everywhere, a useful trick is to match the country of origin of the wine with the country of origin of the food.

Breton oysters go perfectly with Muscadet de Sèvre et Maine.

Starters and snacks

Neutral whites are good with Caesar salad, carpaccio, hummus, prawns, prosciutto, salad niçoise, avocado, sushi, dressed crab, taramasalata, whitebait, smoked mackerel pâté, tomato and mozzarella salad, moules marinières, smoked salmon and French onion, seafood, leek and potato, chicken, artichoke and mixed vegetable soups.

Main courses

These wines work well with many different dishes, but here are some of the best accompaniments: cold roast pork, tuna pasta bake, cauliflower cheese, chicken in cream and white wine sauce, chicken Kiev, chicken with tarragon, macaroni cheese, omelettes, fish and chips, fish pie, fish cakes, mussels, kedgeree, langoustines, haddock, herring, fresh and smoked mackerel, hake, sole, red and grey mullet, halibut, bream, plaice, sea bass, prawns, sardines, salmon, scallops, trout, tuna, paella, osso bucco, spaghetti carbonara, seafood pasta, pizza, chicken risotto, chicken pie, cauliflower cheese, gammon, quiche, quail, roast chicken, roast pork, saltimbocca, guinea fowl and spinach and ricotta lasagne.

Portuguese wine regions
It can be difficult to get to grips with
Portuguese wine if you live on a diet
of Aussie Chardonnay. For a start,
the labels are meaningless unless
you speak the lingo. Secondly, most
Portuguese wines are made from
indigenous grape varieties. But do
not be frightened of these strange
names – they offer a unique
spectrum of hugely enjoyable and
refreshingly different flavours.

VINHO
VERDE

DOURO

Oporto
(Porto)

Tuela

Douro

Mondego

BAIRRADA

DÃO

Coimbra

Tagus
(Tejo)

RIBATEJO

ESTREMEDURA

LISBON
(Lisboa)

SETUBAL

ALENTEJO

ALGARVE

Faro

3 White wines

Country trails

Country	Principal source(s)	Principal grape(s)	Style
Argentina	Cafayate	Torrontés	Aromatic, delicate, highly scented
	Mendoza	Chardonnay (unoaked)	Neutral, crisp, nervy
		Chenin Blanc (unoaked)	Neutral, fruity
		Sauvignon Blanc	Tangy, softer
Australia	Adelaide Hills; Margaret River; Tasmania; Yarra Valley	Chardonnay (oaked)	Richer, bolder, elegant, sophisticated
	Barossa Valley; Clare Valley; Hunter Valley; Margaret River	Sauvignon Blanc/Sémillon blend; Semillon	Richer, bolder, fruitier
	Clare Valley; Coonawarra; Eden Valley; Tasmania	Riesling	Tangy, minerally
	Hunter Valley; Goulburn Valley	Chardonnay (oaked); Marsanne	Richer, bolder, big, sunshine-ripe
	South Australia	Viognier	Aromatic, fruity, floral
	Victoria	Muscat	Aromatic, delicate, highly scented
		Verdelho	Tangy, softer
Austria	Styria	Sauvignon Blanc	Tangy, intense, grassy
	Styria; Wachau	Grüner Veltliner; Pinot Blanc; Pinot Gris	Neutral, fruity
	Wachau	Riesling	Tangy, minerally
		Scheurebe	Aromatic, fruity, floral
Bulgaria	Black Sea	Chardonnay (unoaked); Pinot Blanc	Neutral, fruity
Canada	Niagara Peninsula	Riesling	Tangy, minerally
	Niagara Peninsula; Okanagan Valley	Chardonnay (oaked)	Richer, bolder, elegant, sophisticated
		Pinot Gris	Neutral, fruity
Chile	Cachapoal; Casablanca; Curicó	Chardonnay (unoaked)	Neutral, crisp, nervy

Country trails

Country	Principal source(s)	Principal grape(s)	Style
	Casablanca Valley	Sauvignon Blanc	Tangy, softer
England	South	Bacchus; Huxelrebe	Tangy, intense, grassy
		Schönburger	Aromatic, fruity, floral
France	Alsace	Gewürztraminer	Aromatic, pungent
	Alsace; Loire	Chenin Blanc (unoaked); Pinot Blanc; Pinot Gris	Neutral, fruity
		Chenin Blanc (unoaked); Riesling	Tangy, minerally
	Alsace; Vin de Pays d'Oc	Muscat	Aromatic, delicate, highly scented
	Bergerac; Bordeaux; Loire; southwest	Colombard; Sauvignon Blanc	Tangy, softer
	Bordeaux; Loire	Chenin Blanc (oaked); Sauvignon Blanc/Sémillon blend	Richer, bolder, fruitier
	Burgundy	Chardonnay (oaked)	Richer, bolder, elegant, sophisticated
	Burgundy; Loire; Vin de Pays d'Oc	Aligoté; Chardonnay (unoaked); Melon de Bourgogne	Neutral, crisp, nervy
	Loire	Sauvignon Blanc	Tangy, intense, grassy
	Rhône	Viognier	Aromatic, fruity, floral
Germany	Baden; Pfalz	Grauburgunder	Neutral, fruity
	Baden; Pfalz; Mosel-Saar-Ruwer; Nahe; Rheingau; Rheinhessen	Riesling	Tangy, minerally
	Baden; Pfalz; Sachsen; Württemberg	Gewürztraminer	Aromatic, pungent
	Everywhere	Scheurebe	Aromatic, fruity, floral
Greece	Santorini	Assyrtiko	Tangy, intense, grassy
Hungary	Balatonboglar	Irsai Olivér; Hárslevelü;	Aromatic, delicate,

Country trails

Country	Principal source(s)	Principal grape(s)	Style
		Leányka	highly scented
	Eger; Skekszárd; Siklós	Chardonnay (unoaked); Pinot Blanc	Neutral, fruity
	Mátraalja; Mór	Sauvignon Blanc	Tangy, intense, grassy
	Villány-Siklós	Gewürztraminer	Aromatic, pungent
Italy	Campania; Emilia-Romagna; Lazio; Lombardia; Marche; Piemonte; Puglia; Umbria; Tuscany; Veneto	Various, mainly Trebbiano-based indigenous blends]	Neutral, nutty-edged
	Friuli-Venezia Giulia; Sicily; Trentino-Alto Adige; Tuscany	Chardonnay (unoaked); Pinot Blanc; Pinot Grigio	Neutral, fruity
	Friuli-Venezia Giulia; Trentino-Alto Adige	Chardonnay (unoaked); Vermentino; Vernaccia	Neutral, crisp, nervy
		Gewürztraminer	Aromatic, pungent
		Sauvignon Blanc	Tangy, softer
New Zealand	Canterbury; Marlborough; Nelson	Chardonnay (oaked)	Richer, bolder, elegant, sophisticated
	Central Otago	Pinot Gris	Neutral, fruity
	Everywhere	Chardonnay (unoaked)	Neutral, crisp, nervy
	Marlborough	Sauvignon Blanc	Tangy, intense, grassy
	Marlborough; Nelson	Riesling	Tangy, minerally
	Martinborough	Gewürztraminer	Aromatic, pungent
	North Island	Sauvignon Blanc (oaked)	Richer, bolder, fruitier
Portugal	Central; south	Arinto	Tangy, intense, grassy
	Vinho Verde	Alvarinho/Arinto/Escagna Cão/ Loureiro/ Trajadura blend	Neutral, crisp, nervy
South Africa	Constantia; Elgin; Robertson	Sauvignon Blanc	Tangy, intense, grassy
	Everywhere	Chardonnay (unoaked)	Neutral, crisp, nervy

Country	Principal source(s)	Principal grape(s)	Style
		Chenin Blanc (unoaked)	Neutral, fruity
		Colombard	Tangy, softer
	Paarl	Chenin Blanc (oaked)	Richer, bolder, fruitier
		Viognier	Aromatic, fruity, floral
Spain	Robertson; Stellenbosch; Walker Bay	Chardonnay (oaked)	Richer, bolder, elegant, sophisticated
	Castilla-y-León	Sauvignon Blanc	Tangy, softer
	Costers del Segre	Chardonnay (oaked)	Richer, bolder, big, sunshine-ripe
	Galicia	Albariño	Aromatic, fruity, floral
	Navarra; Somontano	Chardonnay (oaked)	Richer, bolder, elegant, sophisticated
	Rioja	Macabeo/Garnacha Blanco/Malvasia blend	Richer, bolder, fruitier
Switzerland	Geneva; Valais; Vaud	Chasselas	Neutral, crisp, nervy
USA	California	Chardonnay (oaked)	Richer, bolder, big, sunshine-ripe
		Chenin Blanc (oaked); Sauvignon Blanc (oaked)	Richer, bolder, fruitier
		Gewürztraminer	Aromatic, pungent
		Sauvignon Blanc	Tangy, softer
		Viognier	Aromatic, fruity, floral
	New York State; Oregon; Washington State	Chardonnay (oaked)	Richer, bolder, elegant, sophisticated
		Riesling	Tangy, minerally
	Oregon	Pinot Gris	Neutral, fruity

4 Red wines

There is no doubt that red wines pose a greater challenge compared with other styles. But with that challenge comes the thrill of a multitude of exciting flavours and, dare I say it, a much more interesting drinking experience – as we shall discover in this chapter. If you are new to red wines, it is wise to break yourself into them with an example from the easy-drinking, light-bodied styles ... read on to embark upon the red wine adventure!

How red wines are made

We saw in Chapter 3 how in white wine production the grape juice is separated from the skins as soon as possible. But quite the opposite action needs to be applied in red wine production.

Obtaining the colour...
If you cut a red grape in half, you will observe that the fleshy pulp is transparent and colourless. To make red wine, therefore, the juice needs to remain in contact with the skins so that colour and all sorts of other goodies can be leached out – it is somewhat similar to making a cup of tea, in fact!

...and even more
Both the juice and skins are fermented together and this occurs at a much higher temperature compared with white wines (20°-30°C/68°-86°F) in order to acquire tannin and other vital flavour compounds as well as colour.

Red wine fermentation normally takes four to seven days, though the new wine is usually left on the skins and pips for up to four weeks to draw out extra colour, tannin and flavour. If the winemaker desires even more extract, this is squeezed out by pressing the soggy mass of skins that remains after the wine has been drained off.

One of the great pleasures of good red wine is its vibrant red colour.

Premium wines
As with white wines, premium red styles are matured in oak for anything from six to 18 months or more, very often in brand new barrels in order to maximize all the toasty and spicy characters that new oak offers. In addition, some wines require a period of bottle ageing before they are ready to drink, though with rare exceptions, this is generally the duty of the consumer after they have acquired the wine.

Practical matters

Knowing when to pull the cork from a bottle of red wine can be tricky. But as far as serving temperatures are concerned, you only really need to ensure that the wine is not too cold.

When to drink them

As an extremely loose rule of thumb, inexpensive reds are ready for drinking as soon as you buy them, while a steeply priced bottle may need to be tucked away for many years before it becomes drinkable.

This is particularly true of costly, traditional Old World wines that are described in wine lists as fine wines. Typical examples of this breed hail from places such as Bordeaux, Burgundy and Rhône (all classic French regions). In the New World, however, top wines (and you will know them by their price!) are often highly drinkable in youth, even though the label states that they may be kept.

Serve it at the right temperature

Warm temperatures bring out the fruitiness in red wines and make them easier to drink. The richer the style, the warmer it should be – though no red wine tastes good above 20°C /68°F. Note, however, that many light-bodied reds, such as Tarrango and simple Beaujolais, often profit from being lightly chilled, especially when the weather is hot.

Ideal serving temperatures		
Style	**Example**	**Temperature**
Easy-drinking	Beaujolais (France)	11°-13°C/52°-55°F
Overtly fruity	Red Bordeaux (France)	14°-18°C/57°-64°F
Mellow	Red Burgundy (France)	15°-17°C/59°-63°F
Powerful	Australian Shiraz	17°-20°C/63°-68°F

Decanting wine

When you view old black and white movies where the characters, dressed up to the nines, are seated around a long, well-dressed dining table, you rarely see an actual bottle of wine residing on the sideboard, do you? Instead, every drop that anyone drinks is served from a decanter.

Decanting avoids the unpleasantness of finding sediment in your glass.

So do we still need to decant wine?

The answer to this is both yes and no. Many premium wines throw a deposit during their period of bottle maturation and decanting will therefore become necessary – the main reason for decanting is to separate the wine from this sludge. The majority of wines, however, do not need to be decanted because they are made in such a way that they do not require any bottle ageing and will therefore not develop any sediment in the bottle. Having said that, aesthetically all wines look good served in a decanter – even white wines.

Another breath of fresh air

A beneficial side-effect of decanting is that it exposes the wine to air, which helps to bring out its aromas and flavours. It follows, therefore, that you can put your decanter to excellent use for those emergencies when it turns out that a red wine is too young when you pop its cork – and mouth-puckering tannin is the big giveaway here (think of accidentally drinking tea leaves; it is exactly the same effect). The best way of dealing with this problem is to aerate the wine. All you need to do is to empty it into a decanter, carafe or jug, creating as much froth as you can by pouring it from a height and by giving the container a vigorous shake or three afterwards.

How to decant

Stand the bottle upright for 24 hours to allow the sediment to slide to the bottom of the bottle. The next step is to remove the cork, but try not to agitate the sediment in doing so – keep the bottle as vertical and as still as possible. If you have a special decanting funnel with an integral sieve, you need only tip the wine through it into your decanter. But do not worry if you do not have such a gadget – it is quite easy to decant without one. Simply direct the beam of a bright torch under the neck of the bottle so that you can see through the glass. Now slowly and continuously pour the wine into the decanter, stopping as soon as you see the sediment racing towards the neck.

Decanting tips

▶ You need only decant wine an hour or two before you intend to drink it.
▶ When decanting white wine, place the decanter in the refrigerator for an hour beforehand.
▶ If you do not want to waste a drop of your precious liquid, strain the dregs through muslin or coffee filter paper.
▶ Washing decanters is made easier if you use soluble denture cleaning powder and a flexible baby's bottle brush (rinsing thoroughly afterwards, of course!).
▶ The easiest way to dry the inside of a decanter is to place it upside down in an airing cupboard.

Whether or not you need to decant wine depends on its style and age. Decanting helps to separate sediment and makes all wines look appetizing.

Easy-drinking reds

Wines in this class vary from the simplest reds in the world to the slightly more serious. Nonetheless, all boast really tasty, juicy, primary fruit flavours and are never demanding to drink.

Light-bodied styles

These are extremely easy-drinking wines, made for immediate consumption, that are very pleasant but are not going to knock your socks off! Fresh, vibrant and sappy in character, these succulent wines burst with the fragrances and flavours of sweet Maraschino cherries, raspberries, banana, red apple, strawberry ice cream, plum jam, redcurrants, bubble gum, kirsch and hedgerow fruit. Sometimes, there is also a pinch of angelica, cinnamon or pepper. Incidentally, they are made from thin-skinned grapes, so they possess little or no mouth-drying tannin – indeed, many people who do not normally enjoy red wines really like this style owing to its lightness.

Typical countries, typical grapes

The best examples are produced from the Gamay grape grown in France's Beaujolais and Loire Valley regions. You can also find these kind of flavours in inexpensive wines made from the following grape varieties: Bonarda (Argentina), Corvina-based blends (Italy) and Schiava (Italy).

Names to look for

If you cannot find the name of the grape variety on the label, then seek out the following names:

- Bardolino (Veneto, Italy) for Corvina
- Beaujolais (France) for Gamay
- Cheverny (Loire, France) for Gamay
- Coteaux de l'Ardèche (Rhône, France) for Gamay
- Lago di Caldaro (Trentino-Alto Adige, Italy) for Schiava
- Rías Baixas (Galicia, Spain) for Mencia
- Valpolicella (Veneto, Italy) for Corvina

Slightly richer styles

Here you can expect all the scents and tastes of the wines mentioned above, but there will be a little more tannin and so they are richer in body and texture. Nevertheless, they remain soft, gluggable wines, intended for everyday drinking.

Typical countries, typical grapes

Once again, we are looking at the Gamay grape and, once again, we are looking at France's Beaujolais region. In this instance, though, the wines are made from grapes grown in vineyards located in individual villages rather than from a blend of grapes grown throughout the region as a whole.

Names to look for

The collective name for these village wines is Beaujolais Crus and to buy them, all you need to do is to hunt down the following village names:

- Brouilly
- Chénas
- Fleurie
- Juliénas
- Morgon
- Régnié
- Saint-Amour

must know

Carbonic maceration
This is a popular, yeast-free method of producing fruity reds with very little tannin. Whole bunches of grapes are placed in a tank under a blanket of carbon dioxide, which creates an anaerobic environment. Fermentation takes place within each berry until they burst, after which a normal fermentation then occurs.

The vineyards of Beaujolais are renowned worldwide.

Easy-drinking reds with food

Light-bodied reds are usually everyday wines that can be drunk at any time. Bear in mind that the majority of them can be drunk chilled, making them ideal for outdoor summertime events.

Starters and snacks

If you are sitting down to hot chicken liver salad, salami or grilled asparagus with goats cheese, then choose a Gamay-based wine – Beaujolais is by far the best for these. It is also a fine partner to a number of soups, most especially pea and ham and French onion.

Main courses

Beaujolais is also a perfect partner to bacon and gammon, moussaka, meat fondue, roast pork, kleftiko, shepherd's pie, oxtail and cold meats. Trade up to a Beaujolais Cru, however, for chilli con carne, cottage pie, kidneys, steak, calves liver and roast beef.

Try Shepherd's Pie with Beaujolais for a great match.

SALTA

Salta

San Miguel
de Tucumán

Catamarca

LA RIOJA

SAN JUAN

Córdoba

Santa Fé
Paraná

Corrientes

**ACONCAGUA
VALLEY**

MENDOZA

Mendoza

**CASABLANCA
VALLEY**

☐ **SANTIAGO**

San Rafael

BUENOS AIRES ☐
Quilmes

**CURICÓ
VALLEY**

**MAIPO
VALLEY**

**RAPEL
VALLEY**

**MAULE
VALLEY**

Concepción

**BIO BIO
VALLEY**

A R G E N T I N A

Mar del Plata

RIO NEGRO

Argentinian and Chilean wine regions
The vast majority of South American wines
are produced in Chile and Argentina, where
progressive producers are now creating
outstanding European-style wines from
international grape varieties. Chile is
primarily red wine territory, though more and
more whites are coming on stream each
year, whilst over in Argentina – the world's
fifth-largest wine producer, incidentally –
some of the best new wave wines are coming
from Malbec and Torrontés, grapes that are
considered Argentine specialities.

4 Red wines

Flavour trails

Style	Country	Principal source(s)	Principal grape(s)
Easy-drinking, light-bodied	Argentina	Mendoza	Bonarda
	France	Beaujolais; Loire; Rhône	Gamay
	Italy	Trentino-Alto Adige; Veneto	Corvina; Schiava
Easy-drinking, slightly richer	France	Beaujolais	Gamay
	Austria	Burgenland	Pinot Noir
Fruity, classic Cabernet Sauvignon/Merlot blends	Argentina	Mendoza	Cabernet Sauvignon/ Merlot blends
	Australia	Everywhere	Cabernet Sauvignon/ Merlot blends
	Chile	Everywhere	Cabernet Sauvignon/ Merlot blends
	France	Bordeaux; southwest	Cabernet Sauvignon/ Merlot blends
	South Africa	Paarl; Stellenbosch	Cabernet Sauvignon/ Merlot blends
	USA	California; New York State	Cabernet Sauvignon/ Merlot blends
Fruity, juicy, black-fruited	Argentina	Mendoza	Cabernet Sauvignon; Malbec; Merlot
	Australia	Barossa Valley; Coonawarra; Margaret River	Cabernet Sauvignon; Malbec; Merlot
	Bulgaria	Everywhere	Cabernet Sauvignon; Merlot
	Canada	Niagara Peninsula	Merlot
	Chile	Curicó; Maipo; Rapel	Cabernet Sauvignon; Malbec; Merlot
	France	Southwest; Vin de Pays d'Oc	Cabernet Sauvignon; Malbec; Merlot
	Hungary	Everywhere	Cabernet Sauvignon; Merlot

Style	Country	Principal source(s)	Principal grape(s)
	Italy	Friuli-Venezia Giulia; Sicily; Trentino-Alto Adige; Veneto	Cabernet Sauvignon; Merlot
	New Zealand	Auckland; Hawkes Bay; Waiheke Island	Cabernet Sauvignon; Merlot
	Portugal	Estremadura	Cabernet Sauvignon
	Romania	Everywhere	Merlot
	South Africa	Malmesbury; Paarl; Stellenbosch	Cabernet Sauvignon; Malbec; Merlot; Pinotage
	Spain	La Mancha; Navarra; Penedès	Cabernet Sauvignon; Merlot
	USA	California; New York State; Washington State	Cabernet Sauvignon; Malbec; Merlot
Fruity, tangy, raspberry-flavoured	Austria	Burgenland	Blaufränkisch
	France	Loire	Cabernet Franc
	Germany	Württemberg	Lemberger
	Hungary	Everywhere	Kékfrankos
	Italy	North-east Italy	Cabernet Franc
	USA	California; New York State; Washington State	Cabernet Franc; Lemberger
Fruity, wild, strawberry-flavoured	Australia	Barossa Valley; McLaren Vale	Grenache; Grenache-led blends
	France	Rhône; Vin de Pays d'Oc	Grenache-led blends
	Portugal	Alentejo; Dão; Douro; Estremadura	Tempranillo
	Spain	Calatayud; Campo de Borja; Cariñena; La Mancha; Navarra; Penedès; Priorat; Ribera del Duero; Somontano; Rioja; Toro; Utiel-Requena; Valdepeñas	Garnacha; Tempranillo
	USA	California	Grenache-led blends

4 Red wines

Flavour trails

Style	Country	Principal source(s)	Principal grape(s)
Mellow, fragrant, juicy	Chile	Bío-Bío; Cachapoal; Rapel	Pinot Noir
	France	Alsace; Loire	Pinot Noir
	Germany	Baden	Spätburgunder
	Italy	Trentino-Alto-Adige	Pinot Noir
	Romania	Dealul Mare	Pinot Noir
	Spain	Penedès	Pinot Noir
Mellow, premium, ageworthy	Australia	Eden Valley; Lenswood; Margaret River; Mornington Peninsula; Tasmania; Yarra Valley	Pinot Noir
	Canada	Niagara Peninsula; Okanagan Valley	Pinot Noir
	France	Burgundy	Pinot Noir
	New Zealand	Central Otago; Martinborough	Pinot Noir
	South Africa	Walker Bay	Pinot Noir
	USA	California; Oregon	Pinot Noir
Powerful, bitter-sweet	Italy	Abruzzo; Marche; Piemonte; Puglia; Tuscany	Barbera; Lagrein; Montepulciano; Negroamaro; Sangiovese
Powerful, dense, long-lived	France	Southwest	Tannat
	Italy	Basilicata; Campania; Lombardia; Piemonte	Aglianico; Nebbiolo
	Portugal	Alentejo; Bairrada; Dão; Douro	Local grapes
	Uruguay	Everywhere	Tannat

Flavour trails

Style	Country	Principal source(s)	Principal grape(s)
Powerful, rich, spicy	Argentina	Mendoza	Syrah
	Australia	Barossa Valley; Clare Valley; Eden Valley; Grampians; Great Southern; Hunter Valley; Margaret River; Mudgee	Shiraz
	Chile	Aconcagua; Colchagua; San Antonio Valley	Syrah
	France	Rhône; Vin de Pays d'Oc	Syrah
	Greece	Nemea	Aghiorghitiko
	Italy	Puglia; Sicily; Tuscany	Nero d'Avola; Primitivo; Syrah
	New Zealand	Hawkes Bay	Syrah
	South Africa	Franschhoek; Paarl; Stellenbosch	Syrah (Shiraz)
	USA	California; Washington State	Syrah; Zinfandel
Powerful, warm, herby	France	Languedoc-Roussillon; Provence	Blends of local grapes
	Spain	Jumilla; Yecla	Mourvèdre

Mellow reds

These gentle, seductive wines are low in tannin, with a supple, velvety quality and a lightish weight in the mouth. Inexpensive versions are full of juicy, upfront fruit, made expressly for early drinking; the more serious styles are global classics that can fetch fortunes at wine auctions.

Aloxe Corton is one of the best-known wine villages of the Burgundy region of France.

Premium, ageworthy styles

For premium and ageworthy, read costly! There is no doubt that this style of wine comes at a relatively hefty price, and though some people would question whether it is worth the outlay, there is no doubt that we are talking here about magical wines of elegance, complexity and finesse. When they are young, they teem with the perfumes and flavours of spring violets, fleshy strawberries and ripe damsons, raspberries and cherries. But as they mature and mellow, they gain curious but stunning, vegetal and savoury flecks of truffles, game, prunes, figs, chocolate, coffee and (even stranger!) autumn leaves and the whiff of a farmyard. Young or old, they are always well-rounded and silky-smooth.

Typical countries, typical grapes

One grape and one region stand out: Pinot Noir and Burgundy in France. Traditionalists argue that well-made red Burgundy can never be replicated, but first class wine is also created to this style in New Zealand (especially in the Martinborough and Central Otago regions) and in California (where the most notable appellations are Anderson Valley, Carneros, Russian River Valley, Sonoma Coast and Santa Barbara

County). Great wines are also emerging from Canada, Australia (in the Eden Valley, Lenswood, Margaret River, Mornington Peninsula, Tasmania and Yarra Valley regions), South Africa (from Walker Bay, in particular) and from other parts of the United States.

Names to look for

Here is that much-played record again ... New World examples always name the grape variety on the label, so Pinot Noir are the words to spot. In France, any red wine labelled Bourgogne must be made from Pinot Noir according to local wine laws, so it is easy to find these wines on the shelves.

If you are aiming for the finest quality, however, then you need to purchase wines that feature Premier Cru, or better still, Grand Cru on the label. These are wines that are produced from grapes grown in the very best vineyards of the Burgundy region.

So what should you buy if your bank balance does not stretch to such starry luxuries? Well, aim instead for a 'village' wine:

- Aloxe-Corton
- Chambolle-Musigny
- Clos de la Roche
- Gevrey-Chambertin
- Givry
- Mercurey
- Nuits-Saint-Georges
- Pernand-Vergelesses
- Pommard
- Saint-Aubin
- Santenay
- Savigny-les-Beaune
- Volnay

In Germany, the Pinot Noir grape is called Spätburgunder.

Fragrant, juicy styles

This is Pinot Noir in another incarnation. These are not wines in which to invest; instead, buy them today to drink today – they are the far more accessible, good value face of Pinot Noir. And the best bit is that they revel in much the same set of flavours – tangy cherry drops, raspberry sorbet, dollops of lush strawberry jam and, not to forget, that luscious lick of Belgian milk chocolate. The major difference is that they do not age well.

Typical countries

Old World wines of this style hail from Austria, France, Germany, Italy, Romania and Spain, in particular. Good everyday Pinot Noir is also made in Chile.

Names to look for

▶ Baden Spätburgunder (Germany)
▶ Bío-Bío (Chile)
▶ Cachapoal (Chile)
▶ Dealul Mare (Romania)
▶ Lago di Caldaro (Trentino-Alto Adige, Italy)
▶ Menetou-Salon Rouge (Loire, France)
▶ Penedès (Spain)
▶ Pinot Noir d'Alsace (France)
▶ Rapel (Chile)
▶ Sancerre Rouge (Loire, France)

Treading wine grapes has a glamorous image, but it is actually back-breaking, exhausting work!

Mellow reds with food

Given their prohibitive cost, most people can only afford to drink premium Pinot Noir on high days and holidays. For this reason, it is worth taking the trouble to cook a really special meal to accompany the finest wines – and, yes, this is one of those occasions when you should cook the food to go with the wine!

Main courses

There are numerous popular main courses from all around the world that work well with these fine wines. Boeuf bourguignon, monkfish, chicken with tarragon, coq au vin, rabbit in mustard sauce, grilled lamb steaks, moussaka, various roasts – chicken, duck, goose, pork and turkey – steak and kidney pie, thick tuna steaks and nut roast ... all these dishes can be matched by inexpensive mellow reds. Serve only the finest, mature styles, however, with beef Wellington, pheasant casserole, roast grouse, partridge, pigeon, quail or venison. Fresh salmon can also work, but generally only with Pinot Noirs from Alsace, the Loire Valley and Oregon.

Boeuf bourguignon is a superb match for any Pinot Noir.

Cheese

New Zealand and Californian Pinot Noir can be happily drunk with Brie and Camembert, which are not always the easiest cheeses to match with wine, especially if they are super-ripe and on the 'turn'. Pinot Noir will also partner some hard cheeses particularly well, including Caerphilly, Cheshire, Lancashire and Manchego. You could also try Vacherin with mature red Burgundy.

Fruity reds

Can aromas and flavours really jump out of the glass? Well, these are the wines that very often achieve this feat! Some are supple, simple and easy-drinking, full of luscious fruit. The expensive ones display a more complex personality and are more demanding in terms of needing years to soften and mellow.

Juicy, black-fruited styles

If you have ever made jam, you will understand what I mean about that satisfying instant when the raw fruit suddenly breaks down into a glorious, gloopy, sugar-bound, simmering mass. As the skin of each berry bursts, the kitchen is flooded with wonderful, taunting, pure fruit smells – and this style of wine offers something similar in the form of freshly-squeezed, sunshine-sweet black fruits, in both aroma and taste.

Coonawarra in south-eastern Australia is home to some of the richest New World reds.

Some wines are jammy, supple and easy-going; others are more serious, thanks to oak ageing which gives complex and

ageworthy stunners with a richer set of smells and flavours –
here there are layers of vivid blackcurrants, blackberries,
plums, mulberries, damsons, Morello cherry, chocolate, green
olives, mint and fruitcake, and, sometimes, bananas and
toasted marshmallows. As these wines age, they acquire a
fragrance of cedar wood, leather, dust, menthol, Marmite,
black pepper, coffee beans and tobacco.

Typical countries, typical grapes

Cabernet Sauvignon and Merlot are the favoured grapes for
this popular kind of wine and because they are so versatile
and easy to cultivate, they pop up almost everywhere in the
wine-making world. Whilst both share a juicy, fruity style,
Cabernet Sauvignon displays more of a cassis character and
greater tannic structure compared with Merlot's plummy
flavours and softer, more mellow personality. While many
cracking wines are created from Cabernet or Merlot alone,
these varieties lend themselves to being blended, either
with each or with other varieties, such as Shiraz. These
blends are discussed elsewhere.

Pinotage, a South African speciality, also produces
exciting wines of this style and is bottled either as a varietal
or as a blend with Cabernet Sauvignon, Cabernet Franc
and/or Merlot. Malbec is another grape that finds its way
into Bordeaux-style blends in southwest France and in
California, Australia, South Africa, Chile and New Zealand. It
also thrives in Argentina, where it is turned into a varietal
wine with spectacular results.

Names to look for

For modern, easy-drinking, fruit-filled quaffers, choose
Cabernet and Merlot from Eastern Europe, Sicily, Spain's La
Mancha and Navarra regions, France's Vin de Pays d'Oc or the
excellent, inexpensive Australian and Chilean examples. Buy

A signpost at
Coonawarra records
the distances to
other famous wine
venues worldwide.

Many top wines hail from the sloping foothills of mountain ranges.

from the following regions if you are looking for long-lived, concentrated, premium versions:

▶ Auckland (North Island, New Zealand) for Cabernet Sauvignon/Merlot blends

▶ Barossa Valley (South Australia) for Cabernet Sauvignon

▶ Colli Orientali del Friuli (Friuli-Venezia Giulia, Italy) for Cabernet Sauvignon and Merlot

▶ Collio (Friuli-Venezia Giulia, Italy) for Cabernet Sauvignon and Merlot

▶ Coonawarra (South Australia) for Cabernet Sauvignon

▶ Estremadura (Portugal) for Cabernet Sauvignon

▶ Friuli Isonzo (Friuli-Venezia Giulia, Italy) for Cabernet Sauvignon and Merlot

- Hawkes Bay (North Island, New Zealand) for Cabernet Sauvignon and Merlot
- Long Island (New York State, USA) for Cabernet Sauvignon and Merlot
- Maipo (Chile) for Cabernet Sauvignon
- Malmesbury (South Africa) for Pinotage
- Margaret River (Western Australia) for Cabernet Sauvignon
- Mendoza (Argentina) for Cabernet Sauvignon, Merlot and Malbec
- Monterey County (California, USA) for Cabernet Sauvignon and Merlot
- Napa Valley (California, USA) for Cabernet Sauvignon and Merlot
- Niagara Peninsula (Ontario, Canada) for Merlot
- Penedès (Spain) for Cabernet Sauvignon and Merlot
- Paarl (South Africa) for Cabernet Sauvignon, Merlot and Pinotage
- Rapel (Chile) for Cabernet Sauvignon and Merlot
- Sonoma County (California, USA) for Cabernet Sauvignon and Merlot
- Stellenbosch (South Africa) for Cabernet Sauvignon, Merlot and Pinotage
- Trentino-Alto Adige (Italy) for Merlot
- Veneto (Italy) for Merlot
- Waiheke Island (North Island, New Zealand) for Cabernet Sauvignon and Merlot
- Walla Walla Valley (Washington State, USA) for Cabernet Sauvignon and Merlot
- Yakima Valley (Washington State, USA) for Cabernet Sauvignon and Merlot

The rich, red soil of Coonawarra produces red wines that are bursting with fruit and flavour.

Classic Cabernet Sauvignon/Merlot blends

For the most part, these are wines that everyone wants to make and everyone wants to buy – indeed, serious money can change hands at auctions for the most eminent examples. They can be complex, powerful beasts, full of beguiling, lush, blackcurrant, plum, redcurrant and bramble fruit, with more than a hint of sweet oak, cedar, pencil shavings and cigar box, and, when made in warm regions, notes of eucalyptus and mint are often evident. Simple, inexpensive wines of this style are made for early drinking, but the finest can be extremely long-lived.

Typical countries

Bordeaux in France is the prime – and most famous – source of this very traditional wine (where it is known as claret). Whilst there is no argument that claret provides the benchmark for this style of wine, seductive lookalikes are created all over the world, the best hailing from just about every wine-making corner of Australia, Chile, South Africa, the United States (especially in California and Long Island) and, increasingly, parts of Argentina. Hopping back to France, other parts of the southwest are home to the more everyday wines of this style.

Clarets can be divided into two camps: wines that are dominated by the Cabernet Sauvignon grape, which are blackcurranty; and those with a blend that relies chiefly on Merlot, which gives a plummier taste. Often, there is a supporting cast in the blend of small amounts of Cabernet Franc, Malbec and/or Petit Verdot, the proportion of each varying from village to village, and from château to

Stacks of wooden cases containing the classic Margaux wine from Château Prieuré-Lichine.

château (which is how estates are named in Bordeaux).

Names to look for

Outside of France, Cabernet Sauvignon/Merlot blends are labelled clearly as such. French versions, however, must be tracked down by specific place names. For budget claret lookalikes from the southwest of the country, look for:

- ▶ Bergerac Rouge
- ▶ Buzet Rouge
- ▶ Côtes de Duras Rouge
- ▶ Côtes du Frontonnais
- ▶ Côtes de Marmandais Rouge
- ▶ Pécharmant
- ▶ Premières Côtes de Blaye Rouge
- ▶ Premières Côtes de Bordeaux Rouge

When it comes to the more expensive versions, Cabernet-led names from France to look for include:

- ▶ Graves
- ▶ Haut-Médoc
- ▶ Listrac-Médoc
- ▶ Margaux
- ▶ Médoc
- ▶ Moulis
- ▶ Pauillac
- ▶ Pessac-Léognan
- ▶ Saint-Estèphe
- ▶ Saint-Julien

Merlot-led names to look for include:

- ▶ Canon-Fronsac
- ▶ Fronsac

Many vines thrive in very rocky soils on steeply terraced mountain slopes.

Tempranillo vines growing on a steeply terraced vineyard in the Douro Valley, Portugal.

▶ Lalande de Pomerol

▶ Lussac-Saint-Emilion

▶ Montagne-Saint-Emilion

▶ Pomerol

▶ Puisseguin-Saint-Emilion

▶ Saint-Emilion

▶ Saint-Georges-Saint-Emilion

Wild, strawberry-flavoured styles

These can be untamed, long-lived wines, packed full of trademark aromas and flavours of squishy-ripe, wild strawberries. You will also find figs, redcurrants, loganberry, blackberries, raspberries, cassis, roasted nuts, vanilla, brown sugar, cocoa, spice, pipe tobacco and a suggestion of bouquet garni leather, earth, white pepper, mud, dust and tar ... quite a mouthful in more ways than one!

Typical countries, typical grapes

Two Spanish grapes produces this style – Garnacha Tinto (aka Grenache) and Tempranillo – so it is not surprising that Spain creates the best wines. Top Tempranillo comes from La Mancha, Navarra, Penedès, Ribera del Duero, Somontano, Toro, Utiel-Requena and Valdepeñas, while Garnacha shines in Calatayud, Campo de Borja, Cariñena and Priorat. And then there is Rioja, which is a blend of the two.

Elsewhere, good Tempranillo is made in Portugal, Grenache is a star of southern France, often as part of a blend with (typically) Mourvèdre, Syrah and Cinsault, and a few wines of this style are now emerging from the New World.

Names to look for

▶ Alentejo (Portugal) for Tempranillo

▶ Barossa Valley (South Australia) for Grenache

▶ Châteauneuf-du-Pape (Rhône, France) for Grenache-led blends

- Côtes du Rhône (Rhône, France) for Grenache-led blends
- Côtes du Rhône-Villages (Rhône, France) for Grenache-led blends
- Dão (Portugal) for Tempranillo
- Douro (Portugal) for Tempranillo
- Edna Valley (California, USA) for Grenache-led blends
- Gigondas (Rhône, France) for Grenache-led blends
- Lirac (Rhône, France) for Grenache-led blends
- McLaren Vale (South Australia) for Grenache
- Santa Cruz Mountains (California, USA) for Grenache-led blends
- Vacqueyras (Rhône, France) for Grenache-led blends

Tangy, raspberry-flavoured styles

These can be striking wines, boasting lashings of raspberries, with blackcurrants, blackberries, red cherries and redcurrants waiting in the wings and, every so often, hints of juicy beetroot, blackcurrant leaf, grass, earth and white pepper. All this is balanced by a bracing, tangy acidity to make the mouth water.

Typical countries, typical grapes

Classic wines of this style are made from the Cabernet Franc grape. It performs best in France's Loire Valley and successful varietal wines are also produced in Friuli-Venezia Giulia and Trentino-Alto Adige in northern Italy, as well as in parts of the New World. Another grapes that creates this kind of wine is the Austrian Blaufränkisch (called Lemberger in Germany and Washington State, and Kékfrankos in Hungary).

Names to look for

The finest Loire wines hail from the following appellations:
- Anjou-Villages Brissac
- Bourgueil
- Chinon
- Saint-Nicolas-de-Bourgueil
- Saumur-Champigny

The relatively cool vineyards of the Loire Valley in France favour the Cabernet Franc grape.

Fruity reds with food

We have seen that fruity reds come in many different flavours and styles. Hardly surprising, then, that they go with a wide range of foods. Wherever possible, match the country of origin of the food to the country of origin of the wine.

Rioja Reserva is a perfect partner to strong hard cheeses.

Starters and snacks

Merlot is the wine to select for cauliflower cheese and warm chicken livers, while a ripe Tempranillo is enjoyable with bean salad, onion tart and chorizo.

Main courses

It is pretty safe to say that any fruity red will go with any meat of any colour, although of course everyone has their own distinct preferences. Merlot, Cabernet Sauvignon (and blends of the two), Carmenère and red Rioja are exceptionally tasty with an array of roasts – partridge, beef, pheasant, chicken, goose, pigeon, duck, pork, lamb and turkey – as well as steak, cassoulet and meat fondue.

Cabernet Sauvignon also partners lamb-based recipes from various cuisines very successfully, such as Irish stew, shepherd's pie and kebabs, as well as pork or beef casseroles, steak and kidney pudding and braised venison. New World Cabernet in particular is great with spare ribs, chilli con carne and other Tex-Mex meat dishes, as is most Spanish Garnacha and Tempranillo.

Cheese

Brie and Camembert need juicy fruity reds – Chilean Merlot or Spanish Tempranillo, for example – while strong hard cheeses work better with mature red Rioja or Saint-Emilion. The latter is also a treat with Gorgonzola.

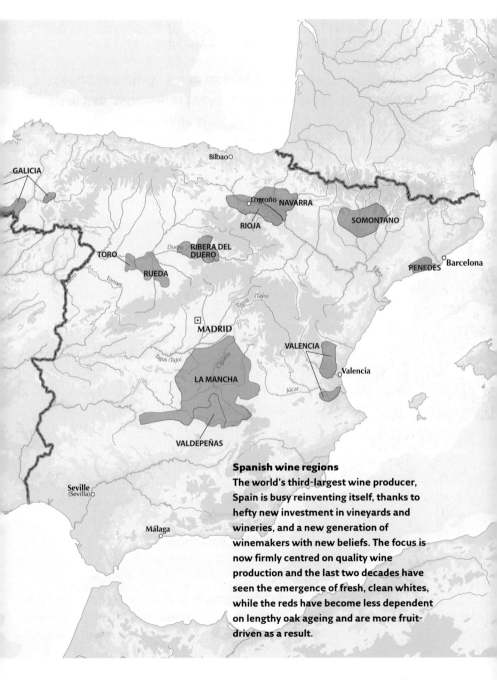

GALICIA

Bilbao

GALICIA

Logroño NAVARRA

RIOJA

SOMONTANO

TORO

Duero

RIBERA DEL DUERO

RUEDA

Tormes

Duero

PENEDÈS Barcelona

Ebro

Tagus (Tajo)

☐ MADRID

Tagus (Tajo)

Cigüela

VALENCIA

LA MANCHA

Valencia

Júcar

VALDEPEÑAS

Seville
(Sevilla)

Málaga

Spanish wine regions
The world's third-largest wine producer,
Spain is busy reinventing itself, thanks to
hefty new investment in vineyards and
wineries, and a new generation of
winemakers with new beliefs. The focus is
now firmly centred on quality wine
production and the last two decades have
seen the emergence of fresh, clean whites,
while the reds have become less dependent
on lengthy oak ageing and are more fruit-
driven as a result.

Powerful reds

Once again, many of the wines that fall into this particular category are much sought after and therefore can be expensive as a result. But equally, there are plenty of bargain wines around, made more affordable because they are either less complex in style, or sport names that are not so well known.

Many powerful, complex red wines are laid down for years in order to mature to their best.

Dense, long-lived styles

These deeply coloured, potent wines are incredibly concentrated, intense and powerful, and are built for a very long life indeed. In youth, they are thick with rich, chewy, mouth-filling tannins, but as they evolve over time, these soften to reveal inviting aromas of herbs, leather, tobacco, dried rose petals, violets, pine, mushrooms, tar and roasting meat, and amazing flavours of stewed prunes, plums, cherries, blackberries, redcurrants, strawberries, raspberries, raisins, vanilla, chocolate and liquorice.

Typical countries, typical grapes

Italy – and most specially its Piemonte region – is a wonderful source of this style of wine, which is made from the Nebbiolo grape (called either Spanna or Chiavennasca locally). But both the Basilicata and Campania regions also turn out wines with these brooding, bruising flavours, this time from the Aglianico grape. Similar blockbuster wines are made in Portugal's Alentejo, Bairrada, Dão and Douro regions from blends of grapes such as Baga, Tinta Barocca, Tinta Roriz (alias Tempranillo), Touriga Franca and

Touriga Nacional. Down in southwest France, Tannat is the grape behind the gutsy black beauties of Irouléguy and Madiran. Tannat is also responsible for creating good, tasty, sturdy and rugged reds in Uruguay.

Names to look for

To buy the very top models of this style, you need to look for the following Italian wines:

- ▶ Aglianico del Vulture (Basilicata) for Aglianico
- ▶ Barbaresco (Piemonte) for Nebbiolo
- ▶ Barolo (Piemonte) for Nebbiolo
- ▶ Boca (Piemonte) for Nebbiolo
- ▶ Carema (Piemonte) for Nebbiolo
- ▶ Falerno del Massico (Campania) for Aglianico
- ▶ Fara (Piemonte) for Nebbiolo
- ▶ Gattinara (Piemonte) for Nebbiolo
- ▶ Ghemme (Piemonte) for Nebbiolo
- ▶ Langhe (Piemonte) for Nebbiolo
- ▶ Nebbiolo d'Alba (Piemonte) for Nebbiolo
- ▶ Roero (Piemonte) for Nebbiolo
- ▶ Sizzano (Piemonte) for Nebbiolo
- ▶ Taurasi (Campania) for Aglianico
- ▶ Valtellina (Lombardia) for Nebbiolo

Warm, herby styles

Lissom and robust, these red wines are strewn with the tantalizing smells and tastes of wild hillside herbs, ripe red cherries, plums and bramble fruit, edged by chocolate, cedar wood and pine needles. Some wines, however, can be more rustic, concentrated and tarry in nature, with touches of spice and liquorice, and hints of spit-roasted meat and the embers of a dying bonfire.

An ancient Syrah vine basks in the warm sunlight of south-western France.

Typical countries, typical grapes

The Languedoc-Roussillon region in southern France is home to this sort of wine and, typically, the wines are made from a blend of different grape varieties – usually any or all of Grenache, Syrah, Mourvèdre, Cinsault and Carignan. In Spain's Jumilla and Yecla regions, wines of this style are made often from Mourvèdre alone (though it is called Monastrell here), giving darker, more powerful characteristics.

Names to look for

As usual, New World versions are clearly labelled by grape variety, and this is also true of Spanish Monastrell. In France, however, you need to unearth the following appellations for the best wines of this style:

▶ Bandol (Provence)
▶ Cabardès (Languedoc-Roussillon)
▶ Collioure (Languedoc-Roussillon)
▶ Corbières (Languedoc-Roussillon)
▶ Coteaux du Languedoc (Languedoc-Roussillon)
▶ Côtes du Roussillon (Languedoc-Roussillon)
▶ Côtes du Roussillon-Villages (Languedoc-Roussillon)
▶ Fitou (Languedoc-Roussillon)
▶ Minervois (Languedoc-Roussillon)

Rich, spicy styles

Whilst there are two types of wine to consider here (very much New World versus Old), many rate in quality alongside the world-famous French Pinot Noirs of Burgundy and the Cabernet Sauvignon/Merlot blends of Bordeaux. When they are first bottled, they are extremely inky and tannic, so they certainly need to be stashed for a few years before they are ready to drink.

As for their aromas and flavours, let us turn to the New World first. Here you can expect to find a unique fusion of the scent of violets, a slap of saddle leather and a niff of smouldering grilled bacon alongside voluptuous, majestic, untamed flavours of sun-drenched blackberries, black cherries, loganberries, raspberries, plus fat, ripe plums, liquorice, sultanas, dates and toffee, all splashed with a twist of black pepper fresh from the mill and a liberal sprinkling of mixed spice. Sometimes there are also hints of eucalyptus, the taste of minty chocolate and more than a suggestion of creosote.

While wines from Old World regions share these sumptuous and complex characteristics, cooler climates mean that they are generally far more austere and restrained, with more of a smoky, peppery, minerally edge, together with powerful touches of wild rosemary and thyme, black treacle, tar and grilled meat.

Typical countries, typical grapes

Shiraz (otherwise called Syrah) is the grape responsible for top wines of this mighty style. Australia produces the archetypal New World model, though terrific versions are also made in Chile, South Africa, New Zealand, Argentina and the United States. In the Old World, France creates the best Syrah, most especially in the northern half of the Rhône Valley and in southern France, and some producers in Italy's Tuscany region are also having a go at it.

Over in Sicily, the Nero d'Avola grape creates smooth, rich, spicy reds oozing dark, stewed fruit,

The Chianti region of Tuscany in central Italy produces some of the Old World's most characterful red wines.

and Greece's indigenous Aghiorghitiko grape gives plummy wines that are very rich and very spicy. Zinfandel (which goes under the name of Primitivo in Italy) is another grape to track down for this turbo-charged style – top Zins hail from California and southern Italy.

Names to look for

As ever, you will always see the names of the grapes on the labels of New World wines of this style; you are less likely to find them on Old World bottles. To this end, you must track down the following place names:

▶ Aconcagua (Chile) for Syrah
▶ Barossa Valley (South Australia) for Shiraz
▶ Clare Valley (South Australia) for Shiraz
▶ Colchagua (Chile) for Syrah
▶ Cornas (Rhône, France) for Syrah
▶ Coteaux du Tricastin (Rhône, France) for Syrah
▶ Crozes-Hermitage (Rhône, France) for Syrah
▶ Dry Creek Valley (California, USA) for Zinfandel
▶ Eden Valley (South Australia) for Shiraz
▶ Edna Valley (California, USA) for spicy Rhône-style blends
▶ Franschhoek (South Africa) for Syrah
▶ Grampians (Victoria, Australia) for Shiraz
▶ Great Southern (Western Australia) for Shiraz
▶ Hawkes Bay (New Zealand) for Syrah
▶ Hunter Valley (New South Wales, Australia) for Shiraz
▶ Lake County (California, USA) for spicy Rhône-style blends
▶ Margaret River (Western Australia) for Shiraz
▶ Martinborough (New Zealand) for Syrah

Tying in the stem of a Shiraz vine in south Australia.

- Mendocino County (California, USA) for Zinfandel
- Mendoza (Argentina) for Syrah
- Mudgee (New South Wales, Australia) for Shiraz
- Napa Valley (California, USA) for Zinfandel
- Nemea (Greece) for Aghiorghitiko
- Paarl (South Africa) for Syrah
- Puglia (Italy) for Primitivo
- Saint-Joseph (Rhône, France) for Syrah
- San Antonio Valley (Chile) for Syrah
- Santa Barbara County (California, USA) for spicy Rhône-style blends
- Santa Cruz Mountains (California, USA) for Zinfandel
- Sicily (Italy) for Nero d'Avola
- Sonoma County (California, USA) for Zinfandel
- Stellenbosch (South Africa) for Syrah
- Tuscany (Italy) for Syrah
- Vin de Pays d'Oc (France) for Syrah

Pruning vines regularly – like any other woody plants – keeps them strong, healthy and disease-free.

Bitter-sweet styles

These are wines with flavours that sound rather horrible on paper. Indeed, is it really possible that wines citing 'bitter' and 'sour' as part of their tasting notes are even drinkable, yet alone enjoyable? Well, yes, to both! A wine such as Chianti is the epitome of this full-bodied style and these can be lovely when carefully made. It should also be borne in mind that this kind of wine is designed to be drunk with food – and we are talking about Italian food, at that. Any astringency in the wine is toned down as soon as you take that first bite.

So, there are touches of bitterness and sourness in this style, but we must not forget the perfume of violets, the bouquet of tinned

tobacco, earth, resin and tea leaves, and all those gorgeous, supple flavours of red cherries, plums, brambles, mulberries, roasted chestnuts, prunes, almonds, strawberries, dark chocolate, redcurrants, raspberries and plump raisins.

Typical countries, typical grapes
Without doubt, Italy is the font of these wines and whilst many are made from a mix of local grapes, very often it is Sangiovese that forms the backbone to the blend. Barbera, Lagrein, Montepulciano and Negroamaro (which translates literally as 'bitter twist') are other Italian grapes that offer this style.

Names to look for
Chianti (from the Tuscany region) has been mentioned above, and for the best flavours that this wine offers, you should buy the superior Chianti Classico, Chianti Colli Fiorentini, Chianti Colli Senesi or Chianti Rufina. Other good Italian wines of this style to seek out include:
► Barbera d'Alba (Piemonte) for Barbera
► Barbera d'Asti (Piemonte) for Barbera
► Barco Reale (Tuscany) for Sangiovese
► Brunello di Montalcino (Tuscany) for Sangiovese
► Carmignano (Tuscany) for Sangiovese
► Copertino (Puglia) for Negroamaro
► Montepulciano d'Abruzzo (Abruzzo) for Montepulciano
► Rosso Cònero (Marche) for Montepulciano
► Salice Salentino (Puglia) for Negroamaro
► Squinzano (Puglia) for Negroamaro
► Vino Nobile de Montepulciano (Tuscany) for Sangiovese

OPPOSITE: **The intense heat of many Spanish vineyards produces powerful, spicy grapes.**

Powerful reds with food

Thanks to their symphony of complex, interesting and exciting flavours, powerful reds can be drunk with an equally complex, interesting and exciting array of powerful foods. However, beware, as this kind of wine can easily overwhelm recipes that call for touches of subtlety and needs to be chosen carefully.

Eat Italian, drink Italian! There is no better companion to prosciutto (Italian ham) than the bitter-sweet Italian reds.

Starters and snacks

For classic Mediterranean starters and snacks, Italian prosciutto, Parma ham and salami are perfect when partnered with Italian bitter-sweet reds. Barbera and Chianti Classico work best of all with these meats.

Main courses

Just about any powerful red is ideal for barbecues, Tex-Mex, nut roast, stuffed peppers, liver and bacon, or beef curry. Everyone has their favourite grapes and styles in this category of wine – as in any other – but to be more specific, Zinfandel is best with fajitas, pheasant, roast beef, stuffed aubergines and oxtail; southern French wines are good with chicken, beef or pork casserole, chilli con carne, sausages, corned beef hash, beef stroganoff and cottage pie; and Aussie Shiraz is perfect for mixed grills, chargrilled chicken with herbs, meatloaf, lamb's liver and coq au vin. Top wines, such as Cornas or Barolo, should be reserved for guinea fowl, pigeon, lamb shanks and rabbit.

Beef lasagne, spaghetti bolognese and meat-filled ravioli, cannelloni and calves liver is suited to Barbaresco, Carmignano; Chianti Classico, Rosso di Montalcino and Vino Nobile di Montalcino, while steaks and roast beef are smashing with Copertino. As a rule, it is fair to say that Italian red wines work best with Italian food.

Brisbane ○

MUDGEE

CLARE
VALLEY

ORANGE

HUNTER
VALLEY

●Perth ○

MARGARET
RIVER

BAROSSA
VALLEY

RIVERLAND

RIVERINA

COWRA

Adelaide ○

McLAREN VALE

EDEN
VALLEY

Murray

CANBERRA □

○ Sydney

YARRA
VALLEY

RUTHERGLEN

PADTHAWAY

COONAWARRA

○ Melbourne

TASMANIA

Hobart

Australian wine regions

Around 90 grape varieties are grown commercially here
– with red grapes comprising over 61 per cent of the
total area under vine – and a diverse range of easy-
drinking wines is made at competitive prices. Given that
Australia has grabbed us by our wine-drinking throats,
you would be forgiven for thinking that the country is
top dog in global terms, yet it enjoys a reputation and
exerts an influence well out of proportion to the
quantity of wine it produces – Australia makes less than
four per cent of the world's wine.

4 Red wines

Country trails			
Country	**Principal source(s)**	**Principal grape(s)**	**Style**
Argentina	Mendoza	Bonarda	Easy-drinking, light-bodied
		Cabernet Sauvignon/Merlot blends	Fruity, classic Cabernet Sauvignon/ Merlot blends
		Cabernet Sauvignon; Malbec; Merlot	Fruity, juicy, black-fruited
		Syrah	Powerful, rich, spicy
Australia	Barossa Valley; Clare Valley; Eden Valley; Grampians; Great Southern; Hunter Valley; Margaret River; Mudgee	Shiraz	Powerful, rich, spicy
	Barossa Valley; Coonawarra; Margaret River	Cabernet Sauvignon; Malbec; Merlot	Fruity, juicy, black-fruited
	Barossa Valley; McLaren Vale	Grenache; Grenache-led blends	Fruity, wild, strawberry-flavoured
	Eden Valley; Lenswood; Margaret River; Mornington Peninsula; Tasmania; Yarra Valley	Pinot Noir	Mellow, premium, ageworthy
	Everywhere	Cabernet Sauvignon/Merlot blends	Fruity, classic Cabernet Sauvignon/Merlot blends
Austria	Burgenland	Blaufränkisch	Fruity, tangy, raspberry-flavoured
		Pinot Noir	Mellow, fragrant, juicy
Canada	Niagara Peninsula	Merlot	Fruity, juicy, black-fruited
	Niagara Peninsula; Okanagan Valley	Pinot Noir	Mellow, premium, ageworthy
Chile	Aconcagua; Colchagua; San Antonio Valley	Syrah	Powerful, rich, spicy
	Bío-Bío; Cachapoal; Rapel	Pinot Noir	Mellow, fragrant, juicy

Country trails

Country	Principal source(s)	Principal grape(s)	Style
	Curicó; Maipo; Rapel	Cabernet Sauvignon; Malbec; Merlot	Fruity, juicy, black-fruited
	Everywhere	Cabernet Sauvignon/Merlot blends	Fruity, classic Cabernet Sauvignon/Merlot blends
Eastern Europe	Bulgaria; Hungary	Cabernet Sauvignon; Merlot	Fruity, juicy, black-fruited
	Hungary	Kékfrankos	Fruity, tangy, raspberry-flavoured
	Romania	Pinot Noir	Mellow, fragrant, juicy
France	Alsace; Loire	Pinot Noir	Mellow, fragrant, juicy
	Beaujolais	Gamay	Easy-drinking, slightly richer
	Beaujolais; Loire; Rhône	Gamay	Easy-drinking, light-bodied
	Bordeaux; southwest	Cabernet Sauvignon/Merlot blends	Fruity, classic Cabernet Sauvignon/Merlot blends
	Burgundy	Pinot Noir	Mellow, premium, ageworthy
	Languedoc-Roussillon; Provence	Mourvèdre or Syrah-based blends	Powerful, warm, herby
	Loire	Cabernet Franc	Fruity, tangy, raspberry-flavoured
	Rhône; Vin de Pays d'Oc	Grenache-led blends	Fruity, wild, strawberry-flavoured
		Syrah	Powerful, rich, spicy
	Southwest	Tannat	Powerful, dense, long-lived
	Southwest; Vin de Pays d'Oc	Cabernet Sauvignon; Malbec; Merlot	Fruity, juicy, black-fruited
Germany	Baden	Spätburgunder	Mellow, fragrant, juicy
	Württemberg	Lemberger	Fruity, tangy, raspberry-flavoured
Greece	Naoussa	Xinomavro	Powerful, dense, long-lived

4 Red wines

Country trails

Country	Principal source(s)	Principal grape(s)	Style
	Nemea	Aghiorghitiko	Powerful, rich, spicy
Italy	Abruzzo; Marche; Piemonte; Puglia; Tuscany	Barbera; Lagrein; Montepulciano; Negroamaro; Sangiovese	Powerful, bitter-sweet
	Basilicata; Campania; Lombardia; Piemonte	Aglianico; Nebbiolo	Powerful, dense, long-lived
	Friuli-Venezia Giulia; Sicily; Trentino-Alto Adige; Veneto	Cabernet Sauvignon; Merlot	Fruity, juicy, black-fruited
	Friuli-Venezia Giulia; Trentino-Alto Adige	Cabernet Franc	Fruity, tangy, raspberry-flavoured
	Puglia; Sicily; Tuscany	Nero d'Avola; Primitivo; Syrah	Powerful, rich, spicy
	Trentino-Alto Adige; Veneto	Corvina; Schiava	Easy-drinking, light-bodied
	Trentino-Alto-Adige	Pinot Noir	Mellow, fragrant, juicy
New Zealand	Auckland; Hawkes Bay; Waiheke Island	Cabernet Sauvignon; Merlot	Fruity, juicy, black-fruited
	Central Otago; Martinborough	Pinot Noir	Mellow, premium, ageworthy
	Hawkes Bay; Martinborough	Syrah	Powerful, rich, spicy
Portugal	Alentejo; Bairrada; Dão; Douro	Blends of local grapes	Powerful, dense, long-lived
	Alentejo; Dão; Douro; Estremadura	Tempranillo	Fruity, wild, strawberry-flavoured
	Estremadura	Cabernet Sauvignon	Fruity, juicy, black-fruited
South Africa	Franschhoek; Paarl; Stellenbosch	Syrah (Shiraz)	Powerful, rich, spicy
	Malmesbury; Paarl; Stellenbosch	Cabernet Sauvignon; Merlot; Pinotage	Overtly fruity, juicy, black-fruited

Country trails

Country	Principal source(s)	Principal grape(s)	Style
	Paarl; Stellenbosch	Cabernet Sauvignon/Merlot blends	Fruity, classic Cabernet Sauvignon/Merlot blends
	Walker Bay	Pinot Noir	Mellow, premium, ageworthy
Spain	Calatayud; Campo de Borja; Cariñena; La Mancha; Navarra; Penedès; Priorat; Ribera del Duero; Somontano; Rioja; Toro; Utiel-Requena; Valdepeñas	Garnacha; Tempranillo	Fruity, wild, strawberry-flavoured
	Jumilla; Yecla	Mourvèdre	Powerful, warm, herby
	La Mancha; Navarra; Penedès	Cabernet Sauvignon; Merlot	Fruity, juicy, black-fruited
	Penedès	Pinot Noir	Mellow, fragrant, juicy
Uruguay	Everywhere	Tannat	Powerful, dense, long-lived
USA	California	Grenache-led blends	Fruity, wild, strawberry-flavoured
	California; New York State	Cabernet Sauvignon/Merlot blends	Fruity, classic Cabernet Sauvignon/Merlot blends
	California; Oregon	Pinot Noir	Mellow, premium, ageworthy
	California; New York State; Washington State	Cabernet Franc; Lemberger	Fruity, tangy, raspberry-flavoured styles
		Cabernet Sauvignon; Malbec; Merlot	Fruity, juicy, black-fruited
	California; Washington State	Syrah; Zinfandel	Powerful, rich, spicy

5 Rosé wines

Pink wines are enjoying a surge of revival in popularity at the moment, and quite rightly so! Without doubt, these are the wines to crack open and quaff on warm spring and hot summer days – there is very little to beat them. While they may appear to be something of a compromise between red wine and white, they share more of the qualities of the latter, though with that extra twist of character.

How rosé wines are made

Many people assume that pink wines are created by mixing red wine with white. However, with just a few exceptions, this is untrue – they are made in a totally different way.

So how are they produced?

As we discussed in Chapter 4, colour is drawn out of red grapes by fermenting and macerating the skins with the juice. Rosés are made by gently crushing the grapes and then allowing the skins to soak in the juice until the desired amount of colour has been acquired – and this often takes only a matter of hours. Some of the tannin and flavour compounds present in the skins are leached out as well, which add extra structure, character and body to the finished wine – but having said that, all rosés are invariably light-bodied in style.

Once the juice has been drained off the skins, it is then treated as if it were a white wine: it is pumped into stainless steel vats where it is fermented at a cold temperature and, when ready, is bottled (and sold!) very quickly.

Decoding foreign terms

You do not need to be a linguist to understand that the words *rosato* (Italian) and *rosado* (Spanish) translate as 'pink'. The Italian term *chiaretto* describes a dark-coloured pink wine and in France's Bordeaux region, some rosés are called *clairet*. Also note that German *schillerwein* is a rosé made from a mix of red and white grapes.

Practical matters

Rosés can be compared to everyday white wines in character and style, and should therefore be treated in exactly the same way. Furthermore, they can often be drunk with the same kind of food.

When to drink them

Rosés are designed to be drunk whilst they are young and fresh – they are definitely 'buy today and guzzle today' kind of wines. They should be fresh, fruity and vibrant in smell and taste – anything less suggests that the wine is tiring, or that it is already past its best. Indeed, whenever you buy a bottle of rosé, the vintage should be your prime consideration, irrespective of anything else. You should aim to drink the youngest rosé on the shelves, so always choose the most recent vintage.

Like white wines, rosés are fermented at cold temperatures in stainless steel vats.

Serve it at the right temperature

Thanks to their light character and fresh, gentle flavours, rosés are more refreshing served cold. If you are drinking them indoors, put them in the door of the fridge for an hour or so to chill down. For summer barbecues, however, when the sun is likely to be beating down, it is worth leaving them in the fridge for even longer – and you could even place them in the freezer until they become icy cool. When you take the bottles out into the garden, keep them in vacuum wine coolers to prevent them warming up too quickly. If you fancy a bottle of rosé with a picnic, always transport it in a cool bag, and if you are on a beach, wrap it in wet towels to help keep it chilly.

Typical flavours

Nine times out of ten, you can be sure that the warmer the climate, the richer and fruitier a rosé will be. For example, rosés from France's relatively northerly and cool Loire region are lighter and more austere than those from the south of the country, where the sun shines more brightly.

Rosé wines are perfect for drinking *al fresco* on warm summer days.

Light, crisp styles

These simple wines – generally from cool climate regions – tend to be very pale in colour, with a fragrant bouquet, refreshing acidity and clean, tangy flavours of rosehips, cranberries, raspberries and crushed redcurrants. Some are dry to taste, while others display a suggestion of sweetness.

Soft, fruity styles

These are produced where the climate is a little warmer, so the wines are deeper in colour, are softer (owing to lower natural acidity) and possess a little more character. Aromas and flavours associated with this style of wine include cream, plums, wild strawberries, blackcurrants and other hedgerow fruits. Most are dry to taste.

Rich, full styles

A warm climate equals riper grapes, richer wines and bolder flavours. You can expect to taste succulent, juicy red cherries, summer pudding, licks of toffee, hints of black pepper and, sometimes, a sprinkling of herbs or spice. Whilst, technically, they are dry, the fruit can often be ripe enough to give an impression of sweetness in the wine.

Blush wines

This style was invented by the Californians in the 1980s and was introduced as an innovative way of marketing rosé wines. At that time, white wine was particularly fashionable in the United States, so many rosés were labelled 'white' even though they were actually pink! White Zinfandel is a prime example, though you may also spot White Grenache and White Merlot. Blush wines are incredibly popular in the States because they are fairly sweet and boast a very slight spritz, but otherwise there is nothing much to recommend them.

Typical countries, typical grapes

Most wine-producing countries make rosé, but the finest hail from Spain and France. Spanish rosados are mainly made from Grenache, whilst in France the focus is on Cabernet Franc, Merlot and blends of Syrah, Grenache and Cinsault. You will also find wines made from Aglianico, Baga, Cabernet Sauvignon, Carignan, Corvina, Dornfelder, Grolleu, Lagrein, Malbec, Molinara, Mourvèdre, Negroamaro, Pinotage, Pinot Noir, Sangiovese, Spätburgunder, Tempranillo, White Grenache and Zinfandel.

Names to look for

With the exception of California (where you should only trust wines created from the Syrah grape), New World rosés are very well made and dependable. In the Old World, however, there is a wide variation in quality and many dodgy (and even disgusting) wines abound. So if you want to spend your money wisely, these are the Old World names to look for:

► Bordeaux rosé (France)
► Cabernet d'Anjou (Loire, France)
► Ciró (Calabria, Italy)
► Lirac rosé (Rhône, France)
► Navarra rosado (Spain)
► Rioja rosado (Spain)
► Rosé de Riceys (Champagne, France)
► Tavel rosé (Rhône, France)

Rosé wines with food

Easy-drinking, refreshing and fruity, rosés are well matched to all the kinds of warm weather dishes you are likely to eat outdoors. Lighter styles are ideal for long, lazy picnics and *al fresco* lunches. Choose a darker-coloured, more robust rosé for barbecues, where the food on offer is more flavoursome or spicy.

watch out!

Rosé wine enemies
Blue cheese and vinaigrette dressings, chutneys, pickles, salsa, horseradish sauce, English mustard, mint sauce and wasabi.

French rosé wines are the perfect accompaniment to rich fish soups such as bouillabaisse.

Starters and snacks

French rosés (especially the ripe and fruity styles from the south of the country, where the sun shines longer and more brightly) lend themselves well to salads – particularly Caesar salad and salade niçoise. These wines are also tasty with crudités, salami, whitebait, avocado with prawns and rich fish soups such as bouillabaisse and lobster bisque.

Main courses

The versatility of rosé wine comes into its own with main courses and it can be served with a whole host of international cuisines (especially Chinese). The key is the fact that so many rosé wines are relatively neutral in taste and will therefore match up with a wide range of different flavours.

Good fish matches include bream, tuna, fresh mackerel, sea bass, cod, trout, red mullet, squid, swordfish, freshly-grilled sardines, seafood risotto and lobster thermidor. But you can also drink it happily with herby chargrilled chicken, moussaka, cold meats, roast rabbit, vegetable couscous, mezze, onion tart, barbecued ribs and Tex-Mex dishes. Rosé is also the drink of choice if you are partial to rabbit braised in cider.

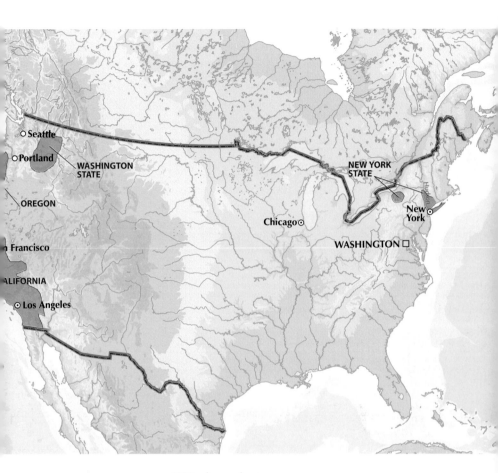

Seattle
Portland
WASHINGTON STATE
OREGON
n Francisco
ALIFORNIA
Los Angeles
Chicago
NEW YORK STATE
New York
Hudson
WASHINGTON □

USA wine regions

While the United States is the world's fourth-largest wine producer, California alone is responsible for some 90 per cent of it, so it is clear that the balance is spread rather thinly across the remaining states. The Pacific Northwest (Washington State, Oregon and Idaho) and New York State are the next most important wine regions and, like California, produce many world-class wines offering subtlety, elegance and complexity. All in all, the USA possesses a wide range of soils and climates, so it is no wonder that there are many separate American Viticultural Areas (AVAs) supporting a diversity of wine styles.

5 Rosé wines

Flavour trails

Style	Country	Principal source(s)	Principal grape(s)
Blush	USA	California	White Grenache; Zinfandel
Light, crisp	Bulgaria	Burgas	Cabernet Sauvignon; Merlot
	England and Wales	East Sussex; South Glamorgan	Dornfelder
	Germany	Ahr; Baden; Pfalz; Rheingau; Rheinhessen; Württemberg	Portugieser; Spätburgunder (Pinot Noir)
	Italy	Puglia; Tuscany; Veneto	Corvina; Molinara; Negroamaro; Sangiovese
	Lebanon	Beka'a Valley	Cabernet Franc; Carignan; Cinsault
	New Zealand	Marlborough	Merlot
	Portugal	Beiras	Touriga Francesca
	Romania	Everywhere	Merlot
Light, crisp (off-dry)	France	Loire	Grolleu
	Hungary	Villány-Siklós	Cabernet Sauvignon; Merlot
Light, crisp (off-dry and spritzy)	Portugal	Bairrada	Baga
Soft, fruity	Argentina	Mendoza	Syrah
	Chile	Most regions	Cabernet Sauvignon; Merlot
	France	Bordeaux; Burgundy; Champagne; Loire	Cabernet Franc; Merlot; Pinot Noir
	Italy	Campania; Sicily; Trentino-Alto Adige; Tuscany	Aglianico; Cabernet Sauvignon; Lagrein; Sangiovese
	New Zealand	Hawkes Bay	Merlot
	Portugal	Estremadura	Periquita

Flavour trails

Style	Country	Principal source(s)	Principal grape(s)
	South Africa	Most regions	Cinsault; Pinot Noir; Syrah
	Spain	Navarra; Rioja; Somontano	Cabernet Sauvignon; Grenache; Tempranillo
Soft, fruity (off-dry)	Argentina	Mendoza	Malbec
	England	East Sussex; South Glamorgan	Pinot Noir
	France	Loire; Provence	Cabernet Franc; Mourvèdre
	South Africa	Most regions	Cinsault; Syrah
	Spain	Penedès	Tempranillo
Rich, full	Australia	South Australia	Grenache
	Chile	Most regions	Syrah
	France	Provence; Rhône; south; southwest	Cinsault, Grenache and/or Syrah
	Italy	Calabria	Gaglioppo
	Morocco	Most regions	Cinsault
	USA	California	Syrah
Rich, full (off-dry)	South Africa	Most regions	Pinotage
	Spain	Penedès	Cabernet Sauvignon

5 Rosé wines

Country trails

Country	Principal source(s)	Principal grape(s)	Style
Argentina	Mendoza	Malbec; Syrah	Soft, fruity (sometimes off-dry)
Australia	South Australia	Grenache	Rich, full
Bulgaria	Burgas	Cabernet Sauvignon; Merlot	Light, crisp
Chile	Most regions	Cabernet Sauvignon; Merlot	Soft, fruity
		Syrah	Rich, full
England and Wales	East Sussex; South Glamorgan	Dornfelder	Light, crisp
		Pinot Noir	Soft, fruity (off-dry)
France	Bordeaux; Burgundy; Champagne; Loire; Provence	Cabernet Franc; Merlot; Mourvèdre; Pinot Noir	Soft, fruity (sometimes off-dry)
	Loire Valley	Grolleu	Light, crisp (off-dry)
	Provence; Rhône; south; southwest	Cinsault, Grenache and/or Syrah	Rich, full
Germany	Ahr; Baden; Pfalz; Rheinhessen; Rheingau; Württemberg	Portugieser; Spätburgunder	Light, crisp
Hungary	Villány-Siklós	Cabernet Sauvignon; Merlot	Light, crisp (off-dry)
Italy	Calabria	Gaglioppo	Rich, full
	Campania; Sicily; Trentino-Alto Adige; Tuscany	Aglianico, Cabernet Sauvignon, Lagrein or Sangiovese	Soft, fruity
	Puglia; Tuscany; Veneto	Corvina; Molinara; Negroamaro; Sangiovese	Light, crisp
Lebanon	Beka'a Valley	Cabernet Franc; Carignan; Cinsault	Light, crisp
Morocco	Most regions	Cinsault	Rich, full
New Zealand	Hawkes Bay; Marlborough	Merlot	Soft, fruity or light, crisp

Country trails

Country	Principal source(s)	Principal grape(s)	Style
Portugal	Beiras	Touriga Francesca	Light, crisp
	Bairrada	Baga	Light, crisp (off-dry and spritzy)
	Estremadura	Periquita	Soft, fruity
Romania	Everywhere	Merlot	Light, crisp
South Africa	Most regions	Cinsault; Pinot Noir; Syrah	Soft, fruity (sometimes off-dry)
		Pinotage	Rich, full (off-dry)
Spain	Navarra; Penedès; Rioja; Somontano	Cabernet Sauvignon; Grenache; Tempranillo	Soft, fruity (sometimes off-dry)
	Penedès	Cabernet Sauvignon	Rich, full (off-dry)
USA	California	Syrah	Rich, full
		White Grenache; Zinfandel	Blush

6 Sparkling wines

From America to Australia, sparkling wines are made in every wine-producing country around the world. Even Belgium can lay claim to a Chardonnay-based fizz from the region of Hainault, a name that obviously extends beyond the end of the Central Line on the London Underground! Not having tasted this particular wine, I cannot personally comment on its quality, but suffice to say that you can expect the best sparklers to originate from countries with a reputation for crafting first-rate wines of other styles.

How sparkling wines are made

There are many ways of creating fizz, but the most superior by far is the *méthode traditionelle* (traditional method). Until the term was outlawed in 1994, this was formerly called *méthode Champenoise* (Champagne method), so named because the technique was developed in the Champagne region of France.

Sparkling wines retain their fizz better when they are served in long tall glasses.

The traditional method

A still wine is produced and blended in the normal manner. The base wine is then bottled and sealed with a crown cap, along with a mixture of sugar, wine and yeast which stimulates a second fermentation. Carbon dioxide, one of the by-products of fermentation, is trapped in the bottle and it is this gas that creates all those tiny, beady bubbles.

As the yeast cells die and sink to the bottom of the bottle, a sediment forms on which the wine rests for many months, gaining extra flavour along the way. The next trick, therefore, is to take the wine off this deposit without losing any of the precious sparkle. This is done by gradually tilting the bottle until it is upside down, which causes the sediment to slip into its neck. The neck is frozen, the crown cap is removed and the plug of frozen sediment shoots out under the pressure of the carbon dioxide. The bottle is topped up with a small volume of sugar solution (a process called dosage), recorked and wire caged, all done as quickly as possible.

Who uses it?

Apart from Champagne, the following wines are made by the traditional method:

- Anything labelled Crémant (France)
- Anything labelled Méthode Cap Classique (South Africa)
- Anything labelled Méthode Traditionelle (anywhere)
- Anything labelled Metodo Classico (Italy)
- Anything labelled Traditional Method (anywhere)
- Blanquette de Limoux (France)
- Cava (Spain)
- Franciacorta (Italy)
- Loire sparklers (France)
- Top New World fizz
- Top quality Sekt (Germany and Austria)

Alternative methods

The transfer method is the second-best way of putting the pop into wine and does away with the time-consuming and expensive component of the *méthode traditionelle*. The secondary fermentation takes place in the bottle, so the wine has the chance to absorb some of the yeasty flavours, but it is then transferred under pressure to large tanks for filtering, dosage and re-bottling.

The ancient cellar at the world-renowned Charles Heidsieck champagne house.

Practical matters

All sparkling wines should be chilled before you open them and not just because it makes them taste better. As to when to open them, it is safe to say that most sparkling wines may be consumed as soon as you buy them.

When to drink sparkling wines

The only style of sparkling wine that demands any serious consideration with regard to potential bottle ageing is Champagne. Vintage Champagne needs to be squirreled away for at least ten years before it reaches its zenith and even a non-vintage version will taste a little smoother if you can resist drinking it for a few months after purchase.

Serve it at the right temperature

Sparkling wines should be chilled to emphasize acidity and to make them less dangerous to open – the warmer the fizz, the faster the cork will fly out.

The key to opening sparkling wine safely is to keep a hand over the cork at all times. Firstly, remove the foil capsule and then drape a tea towel over the top of the bottle. Keeping a firm grip on the cork, unwind and loosen the wire muzzle, but do not be tempted to remove it. Holding tightly onto the cork with the same hand, slowly twist the bottle with the other.

OPPOSITE: **Harvesting the grapes at Champagne Bollinger.**

Ideal serving temperatures		
Style	**Example**	**Temperature**
Rosé	Cava Rosado (Spain)	4°-6°C/39°-43°F
Sweet	Asti (Italy)	4°-6°C/39°-43°F
Dry	Champagne (France)	4°-6°C/39°-43°F
Red	Lambrusco (Italy)	8°-10°C/46°-50°F

Dry sparkling wines

The vast majority of sparkling wines are dry to taste, so as you might predict, there are many different styles from which to choose – and many different levels of quality. As a simple guide, however, the best are made by the traditional method.

A cellarman riddling the bottles in the vast cellar at the Bollinger Champagne house.

Champagne

Champagne is the world's most famous sparkling wine. Over the years, enterprising marketing – and the money to back it – has persuaded us that Champagne is the only thing to drink when we have something to celebrate. In fact, there is truth in this argument, because good Champagne is a luxurious wine and continues to provide the benchmark against which all other sparkling wines are made.

Every Champagne House produces its own signature style, though the balance of the grapes used and the age of the wine also have their role to play. For example, young Champagne tends to be fresh, floral, citrussy and racy whereas more mature wines have developed richer, softer flavours of brioche, hazelnuts and yeast. This is not to say that young wines can never be biscuity, nutty and yeasty, however – much depends on the House style.

Vintage Champagne is in another, far more powerful class altogether. This is velvety, well-balanced wine with true finesse and complex layers of exuberant, opulent, yeasty, creamy, toasty flavours tempered by ripe fruit. Sometimes you can also detect a touch of honey.

Typical grapes

In Champagne, the local *appellation contrôlée* laws permit the use of Chardonnay, Pinot Noir and Pinot Meunier grapes only. Chardonnay provides all the freshness and elegance in the finished wine, Pinot Noir adds backbone, while Pinot Meunier offers fragrance.

Names to look for

The finest Champagnes are made from grapes grown in Grand Cru (the most superior) or Premier Cru (the second-best) vineyards and/or from a single year's crop (Vintage Champagne, in other words, that will carry a year on the label). Note, however, that these prestige styles can be pricey and usually need to be aged.

It is also worth reading the small print on the label. The majority of the big brand names bear the words *négociant-manipulant* (or plain NM) indicating that they are allowed to buy in grapes or wine to create their blends. For more everyday – and often very tasty – styles, look for *coopérative-manipulante* (CM), which are wines made by cooperatives, or *récoltant-manipulant* (RM), which are made by small producers who use grapes from their own vineyards to make their wine.

Flavoursome lookalikes

Champagne is one of the most widely emulated styles of wine in the world and there are plenty of fantastic lookalikes on the shelves at a fraction of the cost of the real thing. The best come from cool climates, giving elegant, creamy wines with subtle, biscuity, nutty aromas and pure flavours of lemons,

Moet & Chandon's distinctive advertising of its Champagne has been famous for decades.

apples, lime cordial and strawberries, rounded off by a delightfully crisp and fresh finish. In warmer areas, the grapes are riper and so hints of pineapple, honey and baked pears tiptoe in and the wine can feel softer yet weightier in the mouth. It is also often slightly sweeter to taste, but in a ripe rather than sugary sense.

Typical countries, typical grapes

Pedigree wines of this style are made from the dream team of Chardonnay and Pinot Noir (the classic Champagne grapes), notably in Australia, New Zealand, California, New York State, Argentina, South Africa and even India! In the Old World, however, the winemaking laws to which we referred earlier often insist upon the use of local grapes, including Riesling, Pinot Blanc, Mauzac and Chenin Blanc – not that this necessarily equates to inferior wines, and they are all worth trying. Another country to keep an eye on is England, which is proving that it can make sparkling wines every bit as good as Champagne – indeed, they have often been mistaken for it.

One of the Charles Heidsieck vineyards.

Words to look for

Remember that top quality lookalikes will always carry one of the following set of words on the label:

▶ *Crémant de* name of region (France)
▶ *Méthode Cap Classique* (South Africa)
▶ *Méthode Traditionelle* (France)
▶ *Metodo Classico* (Italy)
▶ Traditional Method (New World)

Easy-drinking styles

These wines are not in the same league as Champagne, but well made examples can be very pleasant and drinkable indeed. In taste, most are generally neutral and light-bodied in character, but nevertheless offer appealing aromas of pear drops and almonds, and lively, fresh flavours of crunchy green apple peel, lemon drizzle cake and, maybe, some creamy or earthy notes.

Typical countries, typical grapes

Our feet are firmly planted in the Old World here – in Spain, France, Italy, Germany and Hungary. On the whole, these easy-drinking wines are crafted from lesser-known grapes, such as Altesse, Macabeo, Marsanne, Mauzac, Molette, Parellada, Prosecco, Roussanne and Xarel-lo.

Names to look for

The first thing to study is the price of these wines. As a rule of thumb, the easier it is on the purse strings, the harder it is likely to be on the stomach! Digestion-friendly names include:

▶ Blanquette de Limoux (Languedoc, France)
▶ Cava (Penedès, Spain)
▶ Prosecco (Veneto, Italy)
▶ Saumur Mousseux Sec (Loire, France)
▶ Vouvray Mousseux Sec (Loire, France)

Dry sparkling wines with food

It is hard to beat bubbly when we have something to celebrate! Do remember, however, that whilst Champagne is the pinnacle of all sparkling wines, there are many convincing lookalikes that prove a less expensive option for parties. It is also a surprisingly refreshing and invigorating after dinner drink.

Starters and snacks

We tend to drink fizz as an apéritif and yet it is also a delightful accompaniment to many different foods – indeed, the French are happy to drink Champagne throughout the whole meal.

Champagne goes with various starters and snacks, but it is very often an expensive option. So, for more economical options, you could try Australian Sparkling Pinot Noir/Chardonnay with dim-sum, sushi, scrambled eggs, pheasant terrine or avocado and prawns, and Crémant de Bourgogne with taramasalata, smoked salmon, smoked trout or sweetbreads. These are pleasing combinations, but when it comes to caviar, however, only Champagne will do!

Black caviar is best enjoyed with a fine Champagne.

Main courses

Once again, you can save your pennies by drinking Cava or a dry New World Pinot Noir/Chardonnay blend with Chinese food, kedgeree, cold meats (especially beef), soufflé, cold game pie, chicken in creamy sauces, paella, quail, tandoori chicken and rich seafood dishes. If you are eating scallops, crab or lobster, however, this is the time to treat yourself by cracking open a bottle of Vintage Champagne.

Italian wine regions
Vines are found in every Italian province – and probably in every backyard! Only France makes more wine than Italy, though there is barely the thickness of a grape skin between them – in some years Italy beats France in volume. Four regions alone – Apulia, Emilia-Romagna, Sicilia and Veneto – account for 54 per cent of total production (a massive 55 million hectolitres annually, on average). And just to put this into perspective, they each make more wine than the whole of Australia!

STA

TRENTINO
ALTO–ADIGE
Trento

LOMBARDY

Milan
(Milano)

Turin
(Torino)

VENETO

FRIULI–
VENEZIA
GIULIA

Adda

Po

Tanaro

IEMONTE

EMILIA–
ROMAGNA

Reno

EMILIA–
ROMAGNA

Genoa
(Genova)

LIGURIA

Arno

Ancona

MARCHE

Siena

TUSCANY

UMBRIA

Tiber

LAZIO

AMBRUZZO

Aterno

Pescara

ROME
(Roma)

MOLISE

Naples
(Napoli)

Ofanto

PUGLIA

Bradano

Brindisi

SARDINIA

BASILICATA

CAMPANIA

Cagliari

CALABRIA

Palermo

SICILY

Ditaino

SICILY

Sweet sparkling wines

If your last experience of sweet sparkling wine was Italian Lambrusco Bianco, then I would not blame you if you had decided there and then never to drink sweet fizz again! This industrial confection has given sweet sparkling wine a bad name, but there are some wines that rise above this negative image.

Heavenly froth

These dazzling wines – which can be either fully- or semi-sparkling – are gorgeously sweet and frothy, with beguiling scents of tea rose petals, lemon peel, orange blossom, musk and ginger, and scintillating flavours of freshly crushed green grapes, passion fruit and kiwi fruit, alongside touches of sherbet dip. Highly delicate and light-bodied in style, these wines are amazingly refreshing, in spite of their sweetness.

Typical countries, typical grapes
Italy is the main home of this style of wine, which is made from the Muscat grape (called Moscato di Canelli here). Both France and Australia produce the occasional – and very good – Muscat-based imitations.

Names to look for
Asti Spumante is the most popular, fully-sparkling, Italian wine of this style, but make a point of trying Moscato d'Asti, a *frizzante* (semi-sparkling) wine which is far superior. In France, Clairette de Die from the Rhône Valley is the name to look for, though bear in mind that dry versions are also made, so look for the word *mousseux* on the label, which tells you that it is sweet.

Sweet sparkling wines with food

Sweet fizz is a scrumptious dessert wine, especially on those occasions when you are in the mood for a less unctuous, more refreshing style compared with its non-sparkling, sweet white wine cousins. Try one next time you have a special dessert.

Desserts

Rhubarb pie, Christmas pudding, mince pies, fruit kebabs, crêpes suzette, gooseberry fool, tiramisu, jam roly-poly, pavlova, cassata, strawberries and cream, chocolate mousse, pear flan, fruit trifle, baked Alaska, lemon cheesecake, fresh tropical fruit salad, pancakes with lemon and sugar, gâteaux, pavlova, fruit soufflés, light chocolate mousse and roulades ... all these desserts can be safely partnered with Asti, Moscato d'Asti, or any other top quality sweet fizz. These wines are also great with any apple- or raspberry-based puddings.

Break out the Asti with wedding cake if you are looking for a cheaper alternative to Champagne.

Flavour trails

Style	Country	Principal source(s)	Principal grape(s)
Dry – Champagne lookalikes	Argentina	Mendoza	Chardonnay; Pinot Noir
	Australia	South Australia; Victoria; Tasmania	Chardonnay; Pinot Noir
	England	West Sussex	Chardonnay; Pinot Noir
	France	Alsace; Burgundy; Jura; Limoux; Loire	Chardonnay; Chenin Blanc; Clairette; Mauzac; Pinot Blanc
	India	Maharashtra Hills	Chardonnay; Pinot Noir
	Italy	Lombardia	Chardonnay; Pinot Noir
	New Zealand	Marlborough	Chardonnay; Pinot Noir
	South Africa	Franschhoek; Paarl; Robertson	Chardonnay; Pinot Noir
	USA	California; New York State	Chardonnay; Pinot Noir
Dry – easy-drinking	France	Languedoc; Loire; Rhône; Savoie; southwest	Altesse; Chenin Blanc; Clairette; Mauzac; Molette; Muscat
	Germany	Franken; Pfalz; Saar	Chardonnay; Pinot Blanc; Pinot Noir; Riesling
	Hungary	Balatonboglar	Chardonnay; Pinot Noir
	Italy	Trentino-Alto Adige; Veneto	Pinot Grigio; Prosecco
	Spain	Penedès	Parellada; Macabeo; Xarel-lo (sometimes with Chardonnay)
Dry – the real thing	France	Champagne	Chardonnay, Pinot

Flavour trails

Style	Country	Principal source(s)	Principal grape(s)
			Meunier and/or Pinot Noir
Red	Australia	South Australia	Shiraz
	France	Burgundy; Loire	Cabernet Franc; Cabernet Sauvignon; Gamay; Pinot Noir
	Italy	Emilia-Romagna; Piemonte	Brachetto or Lambrusco
	USA	California	Cabernet Sauvignon; Pinot Noir; Zinfandel
Rosé	France	Alsace; Burgundy; Champagne; Loire	Cabernet Franc or Pinot Noir, or Chardonnay, Pinot Noir and Pinot Meunier
	New Zealand	Marlborough	Pinot Noir
	Spain	Penedès	Parellada, Macabeo, Xarel-lo plus Monastrell, Garnacha, Pinot Noir and/or Trepat
Sweet white	France	Rhône	Muscat; Clairette
	Italy	Piemonte	Muscat

Red and rosé sparkling wines

Sparkling wines that possess a little – or a lot – of colour range in style from the serious and sophisticated to the fun and frivolous, yet both fully justify their place in any wine drinker's cellar.

Charming, pink styles

Whether it is rosé Champagne or Cava Rosado, these wines share all the qualities of their paler cousins. The difference is that they possess extra dimensions of aroma and flavour, embracing raspberry yoghurt, wild strawberries, cherries, redcurrants and, sometimes, a hint of freshly-baked patisserie. These added flavours are always quite subtle, so while these wines are definitely more characterful, they remain delicate and silky in style nevertheless.

Typical countries, typical grapes

In France, sparkling pink wines from Champagne and Burgundy gain their colour from Pinot Noir, though Cabernet Franc is the main grape of choice in the Loire Valley. Spain's Cava Rosado is made from the normal trio of grape varieties plus a little Monastrell, Garnacha, Pinot Noir and/or Trepat to provide colour. Pinot Noir is also the grape of choice for most New World pink sparklers.

Names to look for

With the exception of sparkling White Zinfandel from California, most New World versions are very reliable. In the Old World, once again it is Champagne that offers the best quality. Outside of this region, it is important to buy wines that have been made using the traditional method and that are described as Brut. The best styles include:

- ▶ Cava Rosado (Penedès, Spain)
- ▶ Crémant de Bourgogne Rosé (Burgundy, France)
- ▶ Saumur Mousseux Rosé (Loire, France)

Fruity, red styles

Whilst some wines that fall into this category are cloyingly sweet (cheap red Lambrusco comes to mind), these happen to be the ones that should be avoided. The wines to drink instead not only revel in their dryness, but also rejoice in a cocktail of alluring aromas and lip-smacking flavours – dark chocolate, blackberry jelly, blueberries, raspberries, plums, melted treacle, cherries, brown sugar, blackcurrant cordial, chewy liquorice toffees, all lurking behind a vivid purple foam.

Typical countries, typical grapes

Currently, Australia is grabbing the headlines with its trendy sparkling Shiraz. California is also starting to produce a new wave of sparkling reds, crafted from Pinot Noir, Zinfandel or Cabernet Sauvignon. In Italy, Lambrusco and Brachetto grapes have long been used to make highly popular red fizz of the same names, and in France, sparkling reds have long been popular in Burgundy and the Loire Valley.

Names to look for

New World producers' wines are easy to identify. As ever, in the Old World you need to hunt for particular names, the best being:

- ▶ Bourgogne Mousseux Rouge (Burgundy, France)
- ▶ Brachetto d'Acqui (Piemonte, Italy)
- ▶ Lambrusco Rosso (Emilia-Romagna, Italy)

A good sparkling rosé or red wine can make a very refreshing change and clean the palate.

Other sparkling wines with food

With the exception of pink Champagne, perhaps, sparkling rosés and reds are intended to be easy-drinking, fun drinks that should not be taken too seriously. Everyday styles add a definite sparkle to any summer garden party, picnic or barbecue. On the whole, you do not need to worry about specific food matches.

Starters and snacks

A well-made Lambrusco is delicious with Italian antipasti, especially prosciutto and salami. Rosé Champagne is terrific with prawn cocktail and other fishy starters. The subtly flavoured fizz of these sparkling wines definitely enhances snacks or starters that are at all bland in flavour or disappointing in texture.

Main courses

Cava rosado is a suitable choice if you are looking for a less pricey alternative to pink Champagne to drink with fish and shellfish. Meaty dishes such as stir-fried beef in black bean sauce, Peking duck, spare ribs with plum sauce and roast chicken or guinea fowl demand a more robust style of wine, such as Australian Sparkling Shiraz.

Desserts and cheese

Australian Sparkling Shiraz is dreamy with summer pudding and also offers a great match to many chocolate-based desserts. Lambrusco can also be paired with a number of desserts and it also works well with Dolcelatte cheese. Once again, Italian food and wine pairings always come off.

Italian Dolcelatte soft cheese pairs well with sparkling Shiraz.

Country trails

Country	Principal source(s)	Principal grape(s)	Style
Argentina	Mendoza	Chardonnay; Pinot Noir	Dry – Champagne lookalikes
Australia	South Australia	Shiraz	Red
	South Australia; Victoria; Tasmania	Chardonnay; Pinot Noir	Dry – Champagne lookalikes
England	West Sussex	Chardonnay; Pinot Noir	Dry – Champagne lookalikes
France	Alsace; Burgundy; Jura; Limoux; Loire	Chardonnay; Chenin Blanc; Clairette; Mauzac; Pinot Blanc	Dry – Champagne lookalikes
	Alsace; Burgundy; Champagne; Loire	Cabernet Franc; Pinot Noir, or Chardonnay, Pinot Noir and Pinot Meunier	Rosé
	Burgundy; Loire	Cabernet Franc; Cabernet Sauvignon; Gamay; Pinot Noir	Red
	Champagne	Chardonnay, Pinot Meunier and/or Pinot Noir	Dry – the real thing
	Languedoc; Loire; Rhône; Savoie; southwest	Altesse; Chenin Blanc; Clairette; Mauzac; Molette; Muscat	Dry – easy-drinking
	Rhône	Muscat; Clairette	Sweet white
Germany	Franken; Pfalz; Saar	Chardonnay and Pinot Noir, or Pinot Blanc or Riesling	Dry – easy-drinking
Hungary	Balatonboglar	Chardonnay; Pinot Noir	Dry – easy-drinking
India	Maharashtra Hills	Chardonnay; Pinot Noir	Dry – Champagne lookalikes
Italy	Emilia-Romagna; Piemonte	Brachetto; Lambrusco	Red

Country trails

Country	Principal source(s)	Principal grape(s)	Style
	Lombardia	Chardonnay; Pinot Noir	Dry – Champagne lookalikes
	Piemonte	Muscat	Sweet white
	Trentino-Alto Adige; Veneto	Pinot Grigio; Prosecco	Dry – easy-drinking
New Zealand	Marlborough	Chardonnay; Pinot Noir	Dry – Champagne lookalikes
	Marlborough	Pinot Noir	Rosé
South Africa	Franschhoek; Paarl; Robertson	Chardonnay; Pinot Noir	Dry – Champagne lookalikes
Spain	Penedès	Parellada, Macabeo and Xarel-lo (sometimes with Chardonnay)	Dry – easy-drinking
	Penedès	Parellada, Macabeo, Xarel-lo plus Monastrell, Garnacha, Pinot Noir and/or Trepat	Rosé
USA	California	Cabernet Sauvignon; Pinot Noir; Zinfandel	Red
	California; New York State	Chardonnay; Pinot Noir	Dry – Champagne lookalikes

7 Sweet wines

How do you fancy a drop of heaven on earth? These sensational wines are considered gifts from the gods by producers because the very fact that many of them can be made at all relies on nature's bounty rather than the skill of the winemaker. Styles range from fresh and light-bodied styles, full of the scents and flavours of orchard fruits, to deep, dense and powerful wines that can only be drunk in tiny mouthfuls.

How sweet wines are made

Many sweet wines are made by leaving the grapes to hang on the vine beyond the normal harvest date – hence the term 'Late Harvest' – which renders them super-ripe and sweet. Other styles require special natural conditions or use different production techniques to bring out their rich sweetness.

Nature is used to the full in the production of ice wine.

Botrytized wines

Can you imagine wine that has been made from grapes that are left to rot on the vine? Well, as unlikely as it seems, and as long as the rot has been induced by the right kind of fungus (*Botrytis cinerea*), these tiny, shrunken, mouldy-furry berries are responsible for some of the greatest sweet wines on earth. Such grapes, which yield only minute amounts of juice, are so high in natural sugar and acidity that the yeasts cannot work efficiently; it is the unfermented sugar left behind that gives the sweetness.

Ice wine

Here, the grapes are left on the vine until the depth of winter and are picked and pressed only when they are frozen. Because the fruit's water content has turned into ice, only syrupy juice of high acidity and rich extract is expressed and the resultant wine is therefore ultra-sweet to taste.

Passito, Recioto, Vin de Paille and Vin Santo

These are made from grapes sun-dried on mats to increase their sugar levels. As with botrytized wines and ice wines, these berries give up just minuscule quantities of juice when they are pressed in the spring after vintage, which is fermented and aged in small wooden barrels for many years – indeed, some can be positively antique!

Practical matters

Many different styles of sweet wine are embraced in this chapter and each has its own specific demands in terms of when you should drink them and at what temperature.

When to drink sweet wines

As a rough guide, Sauternes, Barsac, ice wine, top Loire and Alsace sweeties and German Beerenausleses and Trockenbeerenausleses are the key styles that need to be cellared, usually for at least ten years, because their development relies on a long period of bottle ageing. These are expensive, so price is a very reliable indicator of whether a wine should be laid down for drinking later.

Other styles can be drunk as soon as you take them home, though Late Harvest New World wines, Recioto della Valpolicella and German QmP wines below Auslese level can be kept for up to five years.

Serve it at the right temperature

If in any doubt, follow the colour code with these wines – the darker the liquid, the warmer the temperature at which it should be served. For example, a pale sweet Riesling should be served icy cold, whilst the darker Vin Santo is best drunk at room temperature.

Decoding foreign terms
In Austria, late-harvest wines that lie between *beerenauslese* and *trockenbeerenauslese* in sweetness are labelled Ausbruch. Other words to indicate sweetness are *moelleux* (France), *liquoreux* and *liquoroso* (Italy and France respectively) and *doce*, *dulce* and *doux* (Italy, Spain and France). South African botrytized late-harvest wines are sometimes called *edel laat-oes* and the German for noble rot is *edelkeur*.

Ideal serving temperatures		
Style	**Example**	**Temperature**
Pale	Riesling QmP (Germany)	6°-9°C/43°-48°F
Golden	Sauternes (France)	9°-10°C/48°-50°F
Dark	Passito (Italy)	15°-20°C/59°-68°F

Typical flavours

Sweet wines contain a lot of residual sugar, which is the wine-speak way of saying that plenty of natural grape sugar is left in the wine after fermentation. This may make them sound rather sticky and cloying, but good sweeties always have a core of tangy acidity to balance the sweetness.

---

must know

Top ten producers
▶ Alois Kracher (Burgenland, Austria) for Scheurebe Beerenauslese
▶ Avignonesi (Tuscany, Italy) for Vin Santo
▶ Brown Brothers (Victoria, Australia) for late-harvest Orange Muscat and Flora
▶ Château Bastor-Lamontagne (Bordeaux, France) for Sauternes
▶ Château Doisy-Daëne (Bordeaux, France) for Barsac
▶ Château d'Yquem (Bordeaux, France) for Sauternes
▶ Disznoko (Hungary) for Tokaji-Aszú
▶ Dr Loosen (Mosel, Germany) for Riesling Spätlese
▶ Horst Sauer (Franken, Germany) for Late-Harvest Riesling
▶ Inniskillin (Canada) for Vidal ice wine

Fresh, grapey styles

These relatively light and easy-drinking whites boast a gorgeous combination of the perfume of orange-blossom and musk, and flavours of crunchy green grapes, lychees and a scratch of candied lemon peel. On the whole, they are very simple wines that do not cost the earth, designed for immediate drinking.

Typical countries, typical grapes

It is the sweet Muscat of Alexandria grape that generates this wine and as we know from Chapter 3, Muscat is the only variety that truly exalts in striking grapey scents and flavours. Spain is the leading source, though you can find this style in Greece and South Africa (where it is frequently labelled Hanepoot).

Names to look for

Specific names to track down are:
▶ Moscatel de Sámos (Greece)
▶ Moscatel de Valencia (Spain)

Late-harvest styles

Made from overripe, sweet grapes, these elegant often minerally wines enjoy a floral perfume and stunning flavours of peach, apricot, pear, apple and quince.

Typical countries, typical grapes

The best wines are made from Riesling in Germany, France, Austria, Switzerland, Canada, Australia, South Africa and the United States. Many producers also weave their magic to create great late-harvest wines from Bouvier, Chardonnay, Chenin Blanc, Gewürztraminer, Grauburgunder (the German name for Pinot Gris), Muscat, Scheurebe (called Sämling 88 in Austria), Tokay-Pinot Gris, Vidal (a hybrid grape) and even Sauvignon Blanc.

Names to look for

For German versions, first look for *auslese* or *spätlese*, which signal that the wine has been made from late-harvest grapes. The next step is to choose a wine from the best villages, namely:

▶ Brauneberg, Erden, Bernkastel, Graach, Piesport and Wehlen, in the Mosel-Saar-Ruwer region
▶ Eltville, Geisenheim, Johannisberg, Oestrich, Rüdesheim and Winkel, in the Rheingau region
▶ Deidesheim, Forst, Ruppertsberg and Wachenheim, in the Pfalz region

There is a range of different wine glasses designed specifically for the consumption of sweet wines.

**Monbazillac is a
classic French
dessert wine.**

Beyond Germany, Austria also uses *auslese* and *spätlese*; in Alsace – the top source of this style from France – these wines are labelled *vendange tardive*; the New World sticks to plain English, that is Late-harvest, followed by the name of the grape; and last but not least, choose eiswein, or ice wine for the ultimate expression of this style.

Super-rich, botrytized styles

Prices can go through the roof for these memorable, long-lived wines, mainly because they cannot necessarily be made every year and production volumes are always pretty low. Nevertheless, if you can find it and afford it, you will relish every sip of this voluptuous, syrupy-sweet nectar, which exudes a cornucopia of flavours.

Typical countries, typical grapes

While the New World makes some sleek and concentrated, golden wines – especially in Australia and South Africa – the finest wines of this style come from Europe. Top sources are France and Germany, though Austria, Switzerland and Hungary make some terrific examples as well. In Germany, Switzerland and France's Alsace region, it is the Riesling grape that shines once again; elsewhere in France, winemakers rely on a blend of Sémillon and Sauvignon Blanc in the southwest of the country and Chenin Blanc in the Loire Valley. Over in Austria and Hungary, Bouvier or Welschriesling and a pairing of Furmint and Hárslevelü are used respectively.

Names to look for

For world-class models of this style, track down the following:
- ▶ Barsac (Bordeaux, France)
- ▶ Beerenauslese (Germany) – choose from the same villages listed under late-harvest styles
- ▶ Bonnezeaux (Loire, France)
- ▶ Coteaux du Layon (Loire, France)
- ▶ Monbazillac (southwest France)

- Neusiedlersee (Austria)
- Quarts de Chaume (Loire, France)
- Sauternes (Bordeaux, France)
- Sélection des Grains Nobles (Alsace, France)
- Tokaji Aszú (Hungary)
- Trockenbeerenauslese (Germany) – choose from the same villages listed under late-harvest styles

Nutty, raisined styles

Deeply-coloured and (quite literally) thick with complex, opulent, intensely sweet flavours of dates, caramelized peaches, dried apricots, brown sugar, honey, toffee, rosehips, nuts, orange peel, coconut, spice ... these are the wines created from those sun-dried, raisined grapes.

Typical countries, typical grapes

A Mediterranean speciality, the best come from all over Italy and from many of the Greek islands. A whole host of local grapes are used to make this style.

Names to look for

Passito, Recioto, Vin de Paille and Vin Santo are the words used around the world of wine to describe this style.

Nutty, raisined wines can be very artisinal, often made in small quantities for the local market.

Sweet wines with food

The sweeter, stickier and more complex the dessert, then the sweeter, stickier and more complex the wine must be for the ideal complement. The key point to bear in mind when choosing companions is that you need to think about matching the wine with the main ingredient in the pudding.

must know

Splash out on the best
If you can afford to push the boat out, Sauternes is the magical golden wine. Sweet Muscat is another terrific all-rounder – Moscatel de Valencia is an excellent choice and will not break the bank.

Try Sauternes with paté de foie gras for a stunning combination.

Desserts

At the end of a good meal – especially on a special occasion when you have plenty of time, such as Christmas Day – it can be fun to break out the dessert wines and just experiment. Sweet Muscat, most especially Moscatel de Valencia, is fantastic with a host of desserts, including profiteroles, Christmas pudding, almond tart, crème brûlée, blackberry and apple pie, gooseberry fool, chocolate mousse, bread and butter pudding, crème caramel, rice pudding, blackcurrant cheesecake and apricot tart. For apple crumble or strawberries and cream, choose an Australian Late Harvest or Botrytized Semillon, Canadian ice wine or a sweet German Riesling. The latter is also tasty with lemon tart and raspberries. Recioto della Valpolicella is best suited to chocolatey Italian desserts. And if you are dishing up blueberry pie, anything goes!

Cheese

German Riesling Spätleses and Beerenausleses combine brilliantly with Wensleydale and Gruyère cheese. On the other hand, Sauternes tastes absolutely wonderful with salty cheeses such as Dolcelatte and Roquefort.

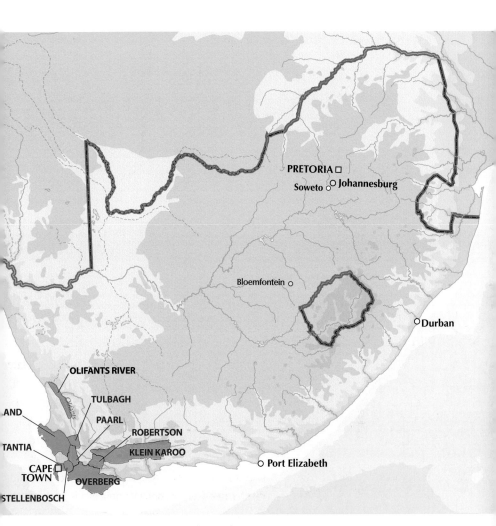

PRETORIA □
Soweto ○ ○ Johannesburg

Bloemfontein ○

○ Durban

OLIFANTS RIVER
TULBAGH
AND
PAARL
TANTIA
ROBERTSON
KLEIN KAROO
CAPE TOWN □
OVERBERG
STELLENBOSCH
○ Port Elizabeth

South African wine regions

South African wines have never been more exciting. Since the end of
Apartheid, this country has raced to catch up with the rest of the
wine world and is now the eighth-largest producer, building on a
legacy dating back to 1652 when Dutchman Jan van Riebeeck planted
the first vines in Cape Town. Even today, most of the vineyards are
located within a 160-kilometre radius of the city, where the
Mediterranean climate is ideal for viticulture. Here, top class grapes
are turned into good value, modern wines of every imaginable kind,
balanced stylistically between the Old World and the New.

7 Sweet wines

Flavour trails

Style	Country	Principal source(s)	Principal grape(s)
Fresh, grapey	Greece	Sámos	Muscat of Alexandria
	South Africa	Olifants River; Worcester	Muscat of Alexandria
	Spain	Valencia	Muscat of Alexandria
Late-harvest	Australia	McLaren Vale; Victoria	Muscat; Riesling
	Austria	Burgenland	Bouvier; Chardonnay; Riesling; Sämling 88
	Canada	Niagara Peninsula; Okanagan Valley	Riesling; Vidal
	France	Alsace	Gewürztraminer; Riesling; Tokay-Pinot Gris
	Germany	Mosel-Saar-Ruwer; Pfalz; Rheingau	Grauburgunder; Riesling; Scheurebe
	South Africa	Worcester	Chenin Blanc; Riesling
	United States	California; New York State	Riesling
Nutty, raisined	France	Southwest	Gros Manseng/Petit Manseng/Petit Courbu
	Greece	Santorini	Assyrtiko; Malvasia/Prugnolo/Trebbiano
	Italy	Tuscany; Veneto	Corvina
Super-rich, botrytized	Australia	Riverina	Riesling; Semillon
	Austria	Neusiedlersee	Bouvier; Riesling; Welschriesling
	France	Alsace; Bordeaux; Loire; southwest	Chenin Blanc; Gewürztraminer; Riesling; Sémillon/Sauvignon Blanc; Tokay-Pinot Gris
	Germany	Mosel-Saar-Ruwer; Pfalz; Rheingau	Riesling
	Hungary	Tokaj	Furmint/Hárslevelü
	South Africa	Worcester	Chenin Blanc; Riesling

Country trails

Country	Principal source(s)	Principal grape(s)	Style
Australia	McLaren Vale; Victoria	Muscat; Riesling	Late-harvest
	Riverina	Riesling; Semillon	Super-rich, botrytized
Austria	Burgenland	Bouvier; Chardonnay; Riesling; Sämling 88	Late-harvest
	Neusiedlersee	Bouvier; Riesling; Welschriesling	Super-rich, botrytized
Canada	Niagara Peninsula; Okanagan Valley	Riesling; Vidal	Late-harvest
France	Alsace	Gewürztraminer; Riesling; Tokay-Pinot Gris	Late-harvest
	Alsace; Bordeaux; Loire; southwest	Chenin Blanc; Gewürztraminer; Riesling; Sémillon/Sauvignon Blanc; Tokay-Pinot Gris	Super-rich, botrytized
	Southwest	Gros Manseng/Petit Manseng/Petit Courbu	Nutty, raisined
Germany	Mosel-Saar-Ruwer; Pfalz; Rheingau	Grauburgunder; Riesling; Scheurebe	Late-harvest
		Riesling	Super-rich, botrytized
Greece	Sámos	Muscat of Alexandria	Fresh, grapey
	Santorini	Assyrtiko; Malvasia/Prugnolo/Trebbiano	Nutty, raisined
Hungary	Tokaj	Furmint/Hárslevelü	Super-rich, botrytized
Italy	Tuscany; Veneto	Corvina	Nutty, raisined
South Africa	Olifants River; Worcester	Muscat of Alexandria	Fresh, grapey
	Worcester	Chenin Blanc; Riesling	Late-harvest
		Chenin Blanc; Riesling	Super-rich, botrytized
Spain	Valencia	Muscat of Alexandria	Fresh, grapey
United States	California; New York State	Riesling	Late-harvest

8 Wine essentials

In this final chapter, we look at the different ways in which you can buy wine, give suggestions on what to purchase if you are starting a wine collection and advise you on how to treat your precious bottles once they are in your home. We also discover how you can exploit your new-found wine knowledge when you are entertaining or are dining out. Last but not least, we examine the health benefits that wine may offer when it is drunk in moderation.

Where to buy wine

There are no rights or wrongs here. You can buy wine from anyone, anywhere, as long as you are happy that you trust your supplier to provide you with decent quality at a fair price.

Supermarkets

Now here is a staggering statistic: in the United Kingdom, the supermarkets account for around 85 per cent of all wine sold. But this is not surprising given that they offer a wide and stimulating range, excellent value (particularly via special promotional deals), a rapid turnover of stock and the convenience of one-stop shopping. The supermarkets have done wonders to demystify wine, so much so that it has now become part of the weekly shopping list, plonked into the trolley together with the washing powder, butter and cat food.

Specialist wine merchants

You will normally find the best selection of wines in a specialist wine shop or off licence.

Head here for top wines, especially if you are seeking expert personal guidance and recommendations from knowledgeable staff who are geared to meeting the needs of the individual.

They are also the chief source of wines from smaller producers who cannot fulfil the volume demands of the supermarkets and larger high-street chains.

The internet

Many well-established mail order wine companies, wine merchants – and even the major supermarkets – now boast on-line services. They are usually very reliable and efficient, and it is easy to compare prices, though keep an eye on potential snags, such as hidden delivery costs and minimum purchase.

Buying 'en primeur'

This is when you buy wine from the new vintage during the spring after the harvest, while it is still in cask and well before it is bottled and shipped 18 months or so later. It is often the only way to secure rare fine wines, but it is risky – the asking price on release may turn out to be less than the sum you paid upfront. Finally, a strong word of advice: always deal with a reputable wine firm, preferably one you have used before and in which you have absolute faith.

Wine auctions

If you are feeling brave and adventurous, a wine auction is the best place to find rare or mature wines, provided you are satisfied with their provenance and condition. It is not necessarily the cheapest means of acquiring them, especially given the buyer's premium which is added to the gavelled-down bid, but it is a thrilling experience!

Buying abroad

Visiting wineries can be exciting and more and more people are incorporating visits into their holidays abroad. Not only do you learn more about wine at first hand, but you may also procure wines that are difficult to unearth elsewhere.

watch out!

Import rules
Depending on where you are travelling to and from, there may be a limit to the number of bottles of wine that you are allowed to import. You should always check carefully and never underestimate the Customs Officer.

Creating a cellar

Statistics record that most wines are consumed within a few hours of purchase. Well, this is most encouraging given that most are made for early drinking, but many are built to last and if you look after them properly, you may save money in the long run.

The building blocks

If you are starting your wine collection from scratch, there is little point in spending your entire budget on wines that are all going to reach their peak at the same time. Instead, you should accrue a range of wines that will mature at different rates and then stagger your purchases thereafter.

Kick off your collection with six bottles each of your favourite everyday white and red wines, a few bottles of fizz and a bottle of port, sherry and dessert wine. This means that you will always have a drinkable wine on hand to suit any event, which you can then replace as and when you get through them.

The next step is to invest in young, finer wines that will be ready for drinking at various stages over the ensuing years. Your choice will be determined by your personal preferences, of course, but try to vary your selection of styles – and only buy wines that you know you like.

How much to buy

When buying wine in bulk, much depends on the size of your cellar – and the depth of your pockets. As a general rule, however, you should think about your average drinking patterns. If, for example, you drink only three bottles of top class red Burgundy over the course of a year, then you could either buy just three bottles to drink when it is at its peak, or, if the wine is expected to stay good for a further four years, then you could lay down a dozen bottles.

Log and review

Many people keep track of their wines on a computer spreadsheet, although a cellar book is equally effective. Whatever you use, it is worthwhile maintaining a record of what you have stashed away, where it is located, when and where you bought it and optimum drinking dates.

It is also advisable to try a bottle from time to time to see how it is progressing (only if you have plenty of the same wine, that is!). Storage conditions vary enormously, so you may find that your wine is maturing at a faster or slower rate than the guides suggest. Also remember that it is always better to drink a wine that is slightly too young rather than one that is past its best.

Is cellaring wine risky?

To be honest, the answer is yes. Sometimes you can nurture a wine for years, only to be hugely disappointed when you crack open the bottle. This may be the result of a faulty cork, or it may turn out to be a simple quirk of nature because each bottle ages slightly differently. Nevertheless, for every disenchantment you experience, there will be myriad rewarding occasions that will prove the merits of cellaring wine.

Cellaring wine is not an exact science, but it can be rewarding.

Tucking it away

Deciding to build up a collection of wine for drinking over the years to come is all very well, but it is also essential to think about how you are going to store it in the meanwhile.

The ideal wine cellar – but probably a little larger than most people will ever own!

Critical considerations

To keep wine in tip-top condition, choose a site that is dark (wine hates ultraviolet light), free from vibration (which can damage fragile styles), well-ventilated (but not draughty) and fairly humid (so that corks stay moist). Of uppermost importance, however, is the ambient temperature of your hidey-hole, which should be between 7°C/45°F and 16°C/61°F – the warmer the temperature, the faster the wine will mature. What wine craves most, though, is a relatively constant temperature – it does not appreciate wild swings.

Location, location, location

Some lucky people live in houses that possess a chilly, damp, underfloor cellar in which they can salt away their wine. Those of us without such luxuries are forced to improvise. Find the coolest spot in the house – this could be under the stairs, or in a wardrobe, drawers or an empty grate – and insulate the bottles with polystyrene, cardboard or blankets to protect them from unstable temperatures.

Steer clear of garages, roof spaces, garden sheds and kitchens as they tend to be unsuitable environments – too cold, too warm, or the temperature fluctuates too much – and common sense dictates that boilers, cookers, tumble dryers, radiators, hot water pipes and windowsills should be avoided at all costs.

If you have spare space, spare power points and spare funds, buy thermostatically-controlled wine storage cabinets, which house anything from ten to 552 bottles. Alternatively, have a cellar excavated by a specialist firm.

Accessorize

As long as a bottle has a cork in its neck, it is vital that it is stored on its side to prevent the cork drying out and allowing air and bacteria to wriggle in. Wine racks are the obvious solution and come in an assortment of sizes and materials. Some styles allow you to extend your racking as you go along, but if your wine storage area is awkwardly-shaped, investigate made-to-measure designs.

You could also search for wine racks at jumble sales, boot fairs and the like, or store wine in the box in which it was supplied, though cardboard will rot eventually if it remains in prolonged contact with a damp floor.

A humidifier is a great idea if the air is dry, though a simple sponge placed in a bowl of water may do the trick – a far cheaper and easier solution. Other useful gadgets include a minimum-maximum thermometer to monitor temperatures and a can of hair lacquer to spray over the labels to stop them peeling off.

Professional help

When you spend a large sum on wine that needs to be cellared for many years, weigh up the option of using a professional wine storage service in order to guarantee that your purchases are looked after properly. Indeed, this should always be contemplated if you have invested in fine wine intended for re-sale.

watch out!

Bad smells
Another good reason for not storing wine in the garage is that it often harbours a strong whiff of petrol. Wine can be affected by any powerful odour, so do not stash your wine near tins of paint, white spirit or anything similar that could taint it.

Useful gadgets

There is a plethora of corkscrews and wine-related gizmos which are widely on sale, some of them more useful and practical than others. Here is a round-up of my personal favourites.

A foil cutter can take the pain out of opening wine bottles – quite literally!

Screwpull pocket model corkscrew

This is the travel version of the original, patented, self-pulling corkscrew, with the added bonus of an integral folding bottle opener and a cutting blade to remove the foil cap.

The Essential Wine Opener

This rechargeable, battery-powered, cordless corkscrew takes all the effort away from drawing the cork from a bottle of wine. Simply place it over the neck of the bottle, press the button and the cork will be extracted firmly and smoothly in one clean action. Another touch of the button ejects the cork from the corkscrew.

Lint-free linen tea towel

It is the lint-free factor that makes this tea towel so sensible. Reserve it for drying wine glasses only and you will never again be bothered by those tiny strands of material that can ruin the next wine to be poured into the glass.

Drop Stop

If you are forever washing wine-speckled tablecloths, invest in a Drop Stop. It is very easy to use – all you have to do is roll it up and insert it into the neck of the bottle. Reusable.

Foil cutter

After the Screwpull corkscrew, this is my most cherished gadget. Just squeeze and twist and it slices cleanly through the capsule, regardless of the material.

Pink elephant drink coolers

These offer a fun way of keeping your white wine cool on a hot summer's day – and without diluting it! Store them in the freezer until you need them and then pop one or two into the wine as if they were ice cubes. Rinse them off afterwards and return them to the freezer.

Rapid Ice wine cooler

This is one of the fastest methods of chilling down a bottle of wine – and it keeps it cold. Place the sleeve in the freezer until you require it, then slip it over the bottle for five minutes.

Cork retriever

There is nothing more annoying than accidentally pushing the cork into a bottle of wine! This resourceful tool solves the problem of how to rescue it.

Screwpull wine funnel with strainer

This is handy when the colour of the glass of the bottle you are decanting is very dark (which makes it very hard to see through). It also sports a curved spout to promote aeration and comes with a Betamesh filter, said to be the finest filter in the world.

Decanter brush

Cunningly designed to reach into even the most awkward of corners, use this brush to clean any decanter properly and to prevent staining.

Private Preserve wine preserver

This is an ingenious means of keeping opened wine fresh for weeks. Simply squirt a few shots of this tasteless and harmless inert gas mixture into the wine bottle – because it is heavier than air, it sinks to form a blanket of gas over the surface of the wine thus preventing oxygen spoilage.

must know

Finding them
The internet, good department stores and shopping catalogues delivered with your newspaper are the best sources of wine gadgets and gifts. You may also find them in your local wine merchant or supermarket.

There are now some novel corkscrews available on the market, such as the Essential Wine Opener pictured.

Entertaining with wine

Birthdays, anniversaries, Christmas or just having friends round for a meal are perfect excuses to open top quality wines. But you can still have a great time by serving everyday styles, so do not worry if you cannot afford to splash out.

Sizing things up
Magnums (1.5 litres) are practical for parties, as are wine boxes – bag-in-box technology has improved greatly and better quality wines are now being put into them, which is more than can be said for most cartons and cans! The smaller 50cl/37.5cl bottles are the perfect size for dinner party dessert wines.

Posh nosh

The key to successful dinner parties lies in giving your guests a different wine with each course and to do your best to match them to the food you are dishing up. We cannot cover all the variables here, of course, but there are plenty of suggestions within the preceding chapters.

If the budget is tight, one idea is to skip the gin and tonic when your visitors arrive and to offer instead an aromatic white wine such as New Zealand Sauvignon Blanc or German Riesling. The advantage is that you can often continue drinking it with the starter.

Throwing a party

▶ Aim high and cater for at least one bottle of wine per guest.
▶ Buy two-thirds white to one-third red – most people prefer white wines at parties because they are more easy-going.
▶ A choice of three different wines is the norm.
▶ Do not forget to put out water and soft drinks for the drivers.
▶ Agree sale or return with your local drinks store and ask if they will deliver your order.
▶ Also find out if they will lend you glasses.
▶ If you need more glasses, trawl through the charity shops. Will your guests really care if none of them match...?
▶ When glasses have been kept in cardboard boxes, give them a rinse to rid them of any residual smell.
▶ Use the bath to chill large quantities of bottles.

Clearing up afterwards

Whilst it is fine to use the dishwasher to clean everyday glassware, wash decanters and your best glasses in hot water, avoiding detergent, and dry them with a lint-free, linen tea towel. When you put away the glasses, place them upright so that they do not pick up the taint of the shelf. To dispel any moisture lingering inside decanters, simply wedge them upside down in the airing cupboard overnight.

Leftover wines can be dealt with in two ways. Either bung the cork back into the bottle and keep it in the fridge where it will last for a few days – even longer if you decant the wine into a smaller vessel, which reduces contact with air. Alternatively, pour the wine into ice cube trays, or any small container (old yoghurt pots, for example), and freeze it – you will then have a convenient supply of small portions of wine that are handy for sauces, gravies, soups and all those annoying recipes that call for just a tiny amount of wine!

Wine has leavened social – and business – occasions for many centuries.

Restaurant tactics

Ordering wine in restaurants can often be pretty nerve-racking, especially if the waiter is intimidating and hands you a gigantic list bearing hundreds of unfamiliar wine names. So, how do you set about choosing something suitable?

Do not be intimidated by wine waiters and always ensure that you get what you ask for.

Top tips

▶ Ask the wine waiter for help – that is what they are there for, after all. Describe the kind of wine you normally drink and do not be embarrassed about stating how much (or how little!) you wish to spend.

▶ Alternatively, pick a wine that you know you will enjoy, regardless of what you are eating. It will not be the end of the world if you drink Chilean Chardonnay with roast beef!

▶ Try a glass of house wine to see if you like it. If the rest of the wine list appears to be carefully thought out, then the house wine should be reliable. Do not be ashamed about opting for 'only' house wine.

▶ It is only logical to match the nationality of the wine to the nationality of the cuisine.

▶ There is nothing wrong with choosing well-known brands. They become brands because they are popular – and they become popular because they are tasty and well-made.

▶ If you and the other members of your party are all ordering different dishes and want different drinks accordingly, opt for half bottles or wine by the glass.

▶ Whatever you select, always check that you have been given the wine you ordered, make sure that the bottle is opened at the table and never be afraid to send it back if it is faulty.

Wine and health

Many of us imbibe too much alcohol from time to time, even though we are well aware that binge-drinking is bad for us. Basically, heavy drinking is never advisable.

A heartening thought

In spite of the above, there is a growing body of evidence to suggest that a moderate daily dose of alcohol, especially in the form of red wine, is beneficial to health. It can increase resistance to many complaints, from the common cold to cancer, and may also contribute to improved mental ability in old age, especially in women.

So why red wine?

Red wine is considered the thinking person's 'medicinal' drink because it provides so much more than alcohol alone. Grape skins contain organic compounds known as polyphenols, including flavonoids, anthocyanins and resveratrol which act as the antioxidant, anticoagulant 'fat-busters' active in reducing the risk of coronary heart disease and strokes (by lowering 'bad' and raising 'good' cholesterol). As we know, red wine is made by macerating the skins in their juice and the polyphenols are retained, but juice intended for white wine is separated from the skins, so there is little opportunity for the polyphenols to be leached out.

Additionally, it is more usual to drink red wine with food and we are all aware that a good meal lowers the chance of becoming tipsy. A large amount of alcohol is metabolized in the stomach, so if you line it with food, absorption is effectively slowed down.

want to know more?

Take it to the next level ...

- **Food with white wines** – pages 50, 56, 66, 72
- **Food with red wines** – pages 86, 95, 104, 114
- **Food with rosé wines** – page 126
- **Food with sparkling wines** – pages 142, 145, 150
- **Food with sweet wines** – page 162

Other sources
- **Study for a recognized wine qualification with the Wine & Spirit Education Trust. Details of courses worldwide can be found at www.wset.co.uk**
- **When you are next in London, visit the popular Vinopolis wine museum (www.vinopolis.co.uk)**
- **Further excellent information on wine and food matching is available at www.foodandwine matching.co.uk**

Weblinks
- **For information on wine and health, visit: www.winepros.org wine.about.com www.red-wine-and-health.com**

Wine label terms

French wine labels

Appellation d'Origine Contrôlée (AC or AOC) official quality designation that guarantees origin and minimum standards of production.

Assemblage blending.

Blanc white.

Blanc de Blancs wine made solely from white grapes.

Blanc de Noirs wine made solely from red grapes.

Cépage grape variety.

Chai cellar.

Château wine estate.

Claret generic English name for red Bordeaux wines.

Climat an individual vineyard site.

Côte(s) and Coteau(x) superior wines from higher ground. Thus wine from "Côte de X" are better than simple "X".

Crémant fizz made by the traditional method in regions other than Champagne.

Cru literally "growth", meaning a vineyard or group of vineyards of superior quality.

Cru Classé "classed growth"; applies to top Bordeaux wines.

Cuvée the contents of a vat; a blend; or a special batch of wine.

Demi-Sec medium dry.

Domaine wine estate.

Doux sweet.

Edelzwicker a blended Alsatian white wine based mainly on Sylvaner and Pinot Blanc.

Extra-Dry style of Champagne that is sweeter than Brut.

Grand Cru literally "great growth", meaning the best vineyard.

Liquoreux very sweet.

Mas wine estate.

Méthode Traditionnelle term used in Champagne only, describing sparkling wine made by secondary fermentation in the bottle (the best method).

Mis (en bouteille) au Château/Domaine/La Propriété estate bottled wine.

Monopole wholly-owned vineyard.

Mousseux sparkling.

Négociant-éleveur dealer who buys grapes, grape juice and/or wine from various growers, then blends, matures and bottles the finished before selling it under his own label.

Non-Vintage (NV) wine made from a blend of vintages.

Nouveau new wine.

Pétillant semi-sparkling.

Premier Cru literally "first growth", used to describe superior wine villages, vineyard sites or the wines themselves.

Propriétaire-Récoltant owner-vine-grower.

Récoltant vine-grower.

Récolte vintage.

Rosé pink.

Rouge red.

Sec dry.

Sélection de Grains Nobles sweet wine made from classic, 'noble' grapes.

Supérieur wines with a slightly higher alcohol content than is normal for any given appellation. Beware! It does not mean that they are superior in taste!

Sur Lie wines that are bottled directly from their lees without filtering, which adds freshness to the wine.

Vendange Tardive late harvest.

Vieilles Vignes old vines.

Vigneron vine-grower.

Villages selected villages which are considered

superior. For example, "Beaujolais-Villages" is better wine than plain "Beaujolais".

Vin Délimité de Qualité Supérieur (VDQS) the next tier down in quality to Appellation d'Origine Contrôlée (but only occasionally seen).

Vin de Paille golden sweet wine made from dried grapes

Vin de Pays country wines that often offer great character and, usually, great value.

Vin de Table table wine.

Vin Doux Naturel fortified wine made by adding spirit to a wine halfway through its fermentation. This leaves a strong, sweet, grapey-tasting wine that will not ferment any further.

Viticulteur vine-grower.

German wine labels

Amtliche Prüfungsnummer (AP Number) government testing number found on all quality (QbA and QmP) labels that shows that they have passed rigorous laboratory and tasting checks.

Auslese a QmP made from selected bunches of very ripe grapes.

Beerenauslese a lusciously sweet QmP made from individually selected, super-ripe grapes that are usually affected by Noble Rot.

Bereich viticultural district surrounding a village. Bereich Bernkastel, for example, is the area surrounding the village of Bernkastel.

Classic everyday dry white made from a single grape variety and with regional typicity.

Deutscher Landwein country wine that must be trocken or halbtrocken.

Deutscher Tafelwein table wine. Edelfäule German for Noble Rot.

Einzellage individual site, usually preceded by the village name. These wines are considered to be among Germany's finest.

Eiswein a QmP made from grapes picked whilst they are still frozen on the vine. When they are crushed, the frozen water content pops out, leaving tiny volumes of extremely rich,

concentrated, sweet and acidic juice. The resultant wines are extremely long-lived.

Erste Gewächs best vineyard.

Erzeugerabfüllung co-operative bottled.

Grosslage a collection of vineyards.

Gutsabfüllüng estate bottled.

Halbtrocken medium dry.

Hock generic term for all Rhine wines (generally bottled in brown glass).

Kabinett a dry or medium dry QmP made from fully-ripened grapes.

Landwein country wine.

Mild slightly sweeter than halbtrocken, made by adding süssreserve to dry wine before bottling.

Mosel generic term for all Mosel-Saar-Ruwer wines (generally bottled in green glass)..

Perlwein semi-sparkling wine.

Qualitätswein bestimmter Anbaugebiete (QbA) official German quality designation that guarantees origin and minimum standards of production.

Qualitätswein mit Pradikät (QmP) top quality wine "with distinction", progressively classified by natural grape ripeness as Kabinett, Spätlese, Auslese, Beerenauslese, Eiswein and Trockenbeerenauslese.

Rotwein red wine.

Schillerwein pink wine made from a mix of red and white grapes.

Sekt sparkling.

Selection top quality dry wine made from a single grape variety in a single vineyard.

Spätlese a QmP (often dry) made from late harvested grapes that are more intense in flavour.

Tafelwein table wine.

Trocken dry.

Trockenbeerenauslese an intensely sweet, rich and honeyed QmP made from individually selected, super-ripe, shrivelled grapes affected by Noble Rot.

Weingut wine estate.

Weissherbst distinctive, reddish-gold wine made from Spätburgunder.
Winzergenossenschaft co-operative.

Italian wine labels

Abboccato medium sweet.
Amabile slightly sweeter than Abboccato.
Amarone dry wine made from dried grapes.
Annata vintage.
Asciutto bone dry.
Azienda Agricola an estate that produces all of its own grapes (i.e. does not buy grapes from other growers).
Bianco white.
Cantina winery.
Cantina Sociale co-operative winery.
Chiaretto very pale red.
Classico wines that hail from the historical heartland of a wine region. Wines described as "X Classico" are generally considered better than just "X".
Consorzio growers' association.
Dolce sweet.
Denominazione di Origine Controllata (DOC) official Italian quality designation that guarantees origin and minimum standards of production.
Denominazione di Origine Controllata e Garantita (DOCG) the designation reserved for the very best Italian wines.
Fattoria farm.
Frizzante semi-sparkling.
Governo old Italian custom in which dried grapes are added to young wine to induce a second alcoholic fermentation.
Imbottigliato all'origine bottled at source.
Indicazione Geografica Tipica (IGT) country wines, a category often used for top wines that cannot use the DOC designation.
Liquoroso rich and sweet.
Metodo Classico traditional method sparkling wine.
Passito sweet wine made from dried grapes.

Podere smallholding.
Recioto sweet wine made from semi-dried grapes.
Rosato pink.
Rosso red.
Secco dry.
Spumante sparkling.
Stravecchio very old.
Superiore wines with a slightly higher alcohol content than is normal for any given appellation. Beware! It does not mean that they are superior in taste!
Tenuta smallholding or estate.
Vecchio old.
Vendemmia vintage.
Vendemmia Tardiva late-harvest.
Vigna vineyard.
Vigneto vineyard.
Vignaiolo vine-grower.
Vino da Tavola table wine.
Vino Tipico table wine with some regional characteristics.
Viticoltore vine-grower.

Portuguese wine labels

Adega cellar/estate.
Branco white.
Colheita vintage.
Denominação de Origem Controlada (DOC) official quality designation that guarantees origin and minimum standards of production.
Doce sweet.
Engarrafado na origem estate-bottled.
Garrafado (na Origem) bottled (estate bottled).
Garrafeira aged wine.
Indicação de Proveniência Regulamentada (IPR) the next tier down in quality from Denominação de Origem Controlada (DOC).
Maduro mature.
Quinta estate.
Séco dry.
Tinto red.

Velho old.
Verde young.
Vinha vineyard.
Vinho Regional (VR) country wine.
Vinho de Mesa table wine.

Spanish wine labels

Año year.
Blanco white.
Bodega winery.
Cava sparkling wine made by the traditional method.
Cosecha vintage.
Crianza wine aged for a minimum of two years, including at least six months in oak.
Denominacíon de Origen (DOC) official quality designation that guarantees origin and minimum standards of production.
Denominacíon de Origen e Calificada (DOCa) the designation reserved for the very best Spanish wines.
Dulce sweet.
Embotellado (de origen) bottles (estate bottled).
Espumoso sparkling.
Finca estate.
Generoso fortified.
Gran Reserva wine aged for a minimum of five years, including at least two in oak.
Joven young wine with little or no ageing in oak.
Reserva wine aged for a minimum of three years, including at least one in oak.

Rosado pink.
Seco dry.
Tinto red.
Vendemia vintage.
Viña vineyard.
Vino Comarcal (VC) regional wine.
Vino de la Mesa table wine.
Vino de la Tierra country wine.

Other countries

American Viticultural Area/AVA (USA) guarantees origin, but not quality.
Ausbruch (Austria) late harvested.
British Wine (UK) produced in the UK from imported, reconstituted grape concentrate. Not to be confused with English wine, which is made from fresh grapes grown in England.
Cap Classique (South Africa) traditional method sparkling wine.
Cultivar (South Africa) alternative name for a grape variety
Landgoedwyn (South Africa) estate wine.
Meritage (USA) trademarked term that applies to blends of Cabernet Sauvignon/Merlot/Cabernet Franc and Sauvignon Blanc/Semillon.
Schilfwein (Austria) made from dried grapes.
Strohwein (Austria) made from dried grapes.
Süssdruck (Switzerland) off-dry, red wine.
Vintners Quality Alliance/VQA (Canada) guarantees origin and quality.
Wine of Origin (South Africa) guarantees origin, grape(s) and vintage.

Glossary

A

Acidification the addition of acid to the must during alcoholic fermentation, if it is needed.

Acidity natural fruit acids breathe the very life into wine and are essential for zestiness, aroma and balance. Wine would be extremely dull and flabby without them. Generally, grapes grown in cool climates produce wines with higher acidity.

Ageing this takes place in casks and/or bottle and allows the wine to soften and become more mellow.

Alcoholic fermentation the conversion of sugar by yeast into ethyl alcohol and carbon dioxide.

B

Balance a well-balanced wine is one in which sweetness, acidity, fruit, tannin and alcohol are all in perfect harmony.

Barrique 225-litre oak barrel, used to ferment/age wine.

Bâtonnage the stirring of the lees to add extra flavour.

Bentonite type of clay, used as a fining agent.

Blending mixing wines of different style, origins and/or vintages.

Blush very pale pink wine.

Body this is the weight and texture of the wine in the mouth. A rich, 'heavy' wine is termed full-bodied whereas a lighter wine is dubbed light-bodied.

Botrytis cinerea see Noble Rot.

Brut dry.

C

Cap describes the layer of skins floating on the top of fermenting red wine.

Carbonic maceration the alcoholic fermentation of whole bunches of grapes in a vat filled with carbon dioxide. Used to create particularly fruity wines.

Chaptalization the practice of adding sugar to grape juice or must prior to alcoholic fermentation in order to increase alcohol levels in the finished wine.

Co-operative winery belonging jointly to a number of producers in order to pool costs and expertise.

Corked wine affected by 2,4,6-Trichloroanisole. Cross a grape bred from two Vitis vinifera varieties.

Crushing the gentle breaking of the grapes before alcoholic fermentation.

Cryoextraction artificially freezing grapes to remove excess water.

D

Deacidification the practice of reducing the excessive acidity that occurs in cold regions and/or in cold vintages. This is normally carried out by adding either chalk or water and sugar to grape juice prior to alcoholic fermentation.

Density the number of vines planted per hectare.

E

Egg whites used as a fining agent in the production of top red wines. Five egg whites are needed to fine 225 litres of wine.

Egrappage literally "debunching", this term describes the destemming of grapes, a process that takes place after crushing. Grape stems (and stalks) are removed because they cause undesired bitter flavours.

Elevage term meaning "rearing" that describes the number of operations that are carried out between fermentation and bottling (such as clarification, ageing, racking, and so on).

F
Filtering the physical removal of unwanted solids.

Fining the process of clarifying wine by adding a fining agent that chemically removes unwanted solids (proteins, yeasts and other organic particles) held in suspension. These adhere to the fining agent as it sinks through the wine.

Finish also called length, this describes the taste that lingers in your mouth after you have swallowed. Wines with a 'long' or 'good' finish are those where the after-taste persists for some time (a good thing). If the flavour disappears very quickly, the wine has a 'short' finish.

Free-run juice the best quality juice, which runs from crushed grapes before they are pressed.

G
Gelatin animal product used as a fining agent.

Green harvesting the removal of excess grapes to promote the ripening of the remainder.

H
Hybrid a crossing of one vine species with another (usually an American species with Vitis vinifera).

I
Isinglass a protein obtained from the bladders of freshwater fish, notably sturgeon, used as a fining agent.

L
Lactic acid one of the mild acids found in wine, named from lactis, the Latin for milk.

Leaf-plucking the stripping away of excess foliage to allow more sunshine into the canopy.

Lees the yeasty sediment that remains after the completion of alcoholic fermentation.

M
Maceration an important process in red winemaking whereby the grape skins are steeped in grape juice, fermenting wine or new wine to extract colour, tannin and flavour.

Macroclimate the climate of a region.

Magnum bottle size containing 1.5 litres (two normal bottles)

Malic acid a tart, organic grape and wine acid, named from malum, the Latin for apple. It accumulates during the development of the grape, but dissipates as the grape ripens. The malic acid content of grapes grown in cool climates where grapes do not ripen well is therefore much higher than that of very ripe grapes of warmer climates.

Marginal climate where the climate is only just warm enough to permit the ripening of grapes.

Maturation another term for ageing.

Mesoclimate the climate of a small area.

Microclimate the immediate physical environment of a vine.

Must the thick liquid – a mixture of grape juice, stem fragments, grape skins, seeds and pulp – left after crushing.

N
New World generic description for wines from Australia, New Zealand, South Africa, North America and South America.

Noble rot anglicized term for Pourriture Noble, or Botrytis cinerea, whereby a fungus beneficially attacks grapes, causing them to rot and shrivel. This results in concentrated, very sweet juice that is used to make top dessert wines.

Non-vintage (NV) wine made from a blend of different vintages.

O
Oenology the study of wine.

Old World generic term that covers all the

Glossary

traditional winemaking areas of Europe, the Near East and North Africa.

Organic grapes grown without the use of fertilizers, pesticides, etcetera.

Oxidation the over-exposure of wine to air.

P

Pasteurization the sterilization of wine by heating it to a high temperature to destroy yeasts and bacteria. This process is not commonly used, but is a requirement for some Kosher wines.

Phylloxera an aphid that eats Vitis vinifera roots, thus killing the vine. Phylloxera destroyed the majority of European vineyards in the 19th century and is still prevalent worldwide. To protect vinifera vines from this devastating pest, they are grafted onto rootstocks of phylloxera-resistant American hybrid vines.

Pourriture noble *see* Noble Rot.

Pressing the pressing of the grapes to extract the remaining juice.

Pruning: vines must be pruned each year if they are to produce a worthwhile crop of grapes.
Pulp grape flesh.

Pumping over process in which fermenting red wine is pumped over the cap.

R

Racking the transfer of the contents of a barrel into another barrel which helps to aerate the wine.

Residual sugar the unfermented sugars that remain in finished wine, measured in grams per litre. The residual sugar of dry whites and reds measures less than 2g/l.

Reverse osmosis a method of removing excess water from the must.

S

Saccharomyces cerevisiaie the single-celled yeast responsible for turning sugar into

alcohol and carbon dioxide during alcoholic fermentation. While grape skins have a natural coating of wild yeasts, most winemakers use cultivated yeasts because they are more reliable.

Sediment the physical by-products of alcoholic fermentation and of ageing.

Süssreserve unfermented grape juice.

T

Tannin a mouth-puckering substance naturally present in grape skins, stalks and pips (and also found in tea). Tannin is very significant in red winemaking because it adds body and acts as a preservative.

Tartaric acid an important natural acid in grapes and wine.

Terroir each vineyard has its own terroir – a unique 'address' reflecting the interaction between its soil, topography and climate.

U

Ullage the space in the barrel or bottle not occupied by wine.

V

Varietal wine made from (and named after) one grape variety.

Veraison the stage of grape development when it changes colour during ripening.

Vinification the winemaking process.

Vintage year in which the grapes were harvested.

Viticulture concerns anything that happens in the vineyard.

Vitis vinifera the European species of vine used in premium winemaking around the world.

Y

Yeast see Saccharomyces cerevisiaie.

Yield the amount of fruit produced from a vineyard.

Need to know more?

If you are keen to delve deeper into the world of wine, there is a wealth of information available, most especially if you have access to the internet. Listed below are just some of the resources that you may find useful to help you develop your appreciation of wine, but all the major ones are included.

Top wine magazines

Bon Appetit
Decanter
Food & Wine
Quarterly Review of Wines
The Wine Advocate
Wine Enthusiast
Wine International
Wine News
Wine Spectator
Winestate

Gateways to wine websites

There are literally millions of wine websites and it would be impossible to research every single one. These directories therefore serve as good gateways to the best of the world of wine on the web.

www.bboxbbs.ch/home/tbm
www.internetwineguide.com
www.intowine.com/resources.html
www.ryerson.ca/~dtudor/wine.htm
www.wineloverspage.com/winelinks/
   index.shtml

Key generic websites

Visit these websites if you wish to learn more about the wines of a specific country. It is not a comprehensive list, however, because many wine-producing countries have not yet set up a generic website.

Argentina: www.argentinewines.com
Australia: www.wineaustralia.com.au
Austria: www.austria.wine.co.at
Canada: www.canwine.com
Chile: www.winesofchile.org
Cyprus: www.cyprus-wine.com
England: www.english-wine.com;
   www.englishwineproducers.com
France: www.terroir-france.com;
   www.wines-france.com
Germany: www.germanwineestates.com;
   www.germanwines.de; www.wein.com
Greece: www.greekwine.gr;
   www.greekwinemakers.com
Hungary: www.winesofhungary.com
Italy: www.italianmade.com;
   www.italianwineguide.com;
   www.wine.it

New Zealand: www.nzwine.com;
www.winesofnz.com
South Africa: www.wine.co.za;
www.wosa.co.za
Spain: www.jrnet.com;
www.winesfromspain.com
Switzerland: www.wine.ch
USA: www.allamericanwineries.com;
www.appellationamerica.com;
www.winecountry.com

General wine websites

The following websites are the best,
user-friendly – and often highly amusing
– sources of all kinds of general
information on wine. Many offer detailed
reviews and tasting notes of the latest
wines to hit the shelves, interviews with
winemakers, newsletters, reader forums
... and much, much more.
www.erobertparker.com
www.jancisrobinson.com
www.nanson.ch
www.natdecants.com
www.stratsplace.com
www.superplonk.com
www.vines.org
www.wineanorak.com
www.wine-journal.com
www.wineloverspage.com
www.wine-pages.com
www.winestate.com.au
www.winewriting.com
www.winexwired.com

Further reading

The books listed below are essential
building blocks for a wine library.
Beckett, F., *How To Match Food And Wine*
   (Mitchell Beazley, 2002)
Clarke, O. & Rand, M., *Grapes & Wines*
   (Websters/Little, Brown & Company,
   2001)
Johnson, H. & Robinson, J., *The World
   Atlas of Wine* (Mitchell Beazley, 2001)
Robinson, J., *Concise Wine Companion*
   (Oxford University Press, 2001)

Further learning

Joining a wine club or a wine society is
a fun way of enjoying wine with like-
minded people and you can find details
of these in wine magazines, in local
newspapers or on the internet (via a
Google search). If you want to go one
step further, however, why not take an
established wine course? The London-
based Wine & Spirit Education Trust offers
courses at all levels in 28 countries and
eight languages. Further information can
be obtained from:
Wine & Spirit Education Trust,
International Wine & Spirit Centre,
39-45 Bermondsey Street,
London SE1 3XF
Tel: (44) 20 7089 3800
Fax: (44) 20 7089 3845
E-mail: wset@wset.co.uk
www.wset.co.uk

Index

Index

Acknowledgements

The author and publishers wish to thank the following organizations and companies for supplying images for inclusion in this book:

Argiolas; Australian Wine Bureau (UK); Australian Wine Export Council (pages 6, 7, 8, 15, 16, 18, 23, 64, 70, 96, 97, 99); Azienda Livon; Barmans; Birchgrove Products; Bodegas Trapiche; Bollinger (pages 136, 137, 138); Bon Cap; Brand Phoenix; Brown Brothers; Burdin (page 160); Callaghan Communications; Canepa; Carlos Navajas/ICEX (pages 24, 85); Charles Heidsieck (pages 135, 140); Civa (pages 48, 49, 50, 156); Compañia Vinicola del Norte de España; Dolianova; Emma Wellings PR; Ernest & Julio Gallo (page 63); Eric Sander (page 160); Faustino (page 104); Félix Lorrio/ICEX (page 19, 172); Fival (pages 53, 103, 110, 111); German Wine Information Service (UK); IOP (page 102); Graham Beck; Grayling PR; ICEP (UK); João Portugal Ramos; Louis Guntrum; Louis Jadot; Louis Latour; Mentzendorff (pages 136, 137, 138); Moët & Chandon (page 139); Moncaro; New York Wine and Grape Foundation; Newton Stovold; Piper-Heidsieck; Quinta do Crasto; Quinta do Noval; R&R Teamwork; Rocca di Castagnoli; Rust en Vrede; San Simone; Screwpull; Sopexa; Spanish Institute for Foreign Trade (ICEX); Storm Communications; Su-Lin Ong; The Fladgate Partnership; The Rioja Wine Information Centre; The Waiter's Friend Company; The Wine & Spirit Education Trust; Torres; Villa Maria; Waitrose; Warwick Wine Estate (page 98); Weltevrede; Wild Card PR; WineBox; Wines from Spain (UK); Wines of Chile (UK); Wines of Germany (pages 40, 42, 47, 49, 50, 66, 71, 78, 124, 134, 159, 178); Zenato.

☾ Collins need to know?

Look out for these recent titles in Collins' practical and accessible need to know? series.

Other titles in the series:

Birdwatching
Body Language
Card Games
DIY
Dog Training
Drawing & Sketching
Golf
Guitar

Kama Sutra
Knots
Pilates
Speak French
Speak Italian
Speak Spanish
Stargazing
Watercolour

Weddings
Wood-Working
The World
Yoga
Zodiac Types

To order any of these titles, please telephone 0870 787 1732. For further information about all Collins books, visit our website: www.collins.co.uk